A CENTURY
OF NFL
FOOTBALL

A CENTURY OF NFL FOOTBALL

THE ALL-TIME QUIZ

ROGER GORDON

Guilford, Connecticut

An imprint of The Rowman & Littlefield Publishing Group, Inc.
4501 Forbes Blvd., Ste. 200
Lanham, MD 20706
www.rowman.com

Distributed by NATIONAL BOOK NETWORK

British Library Cataloguing in Publication Information available

Library of Congress Cataloging-in-Publication Data available

ISBN 978-1-4930-4459-7 (paperback)
ISBN 978-1-4930-4460-3 (e-book)

♾™ The paper used in this publication meets the minimum requirements of American National Standard for Information Sciences—Permanence of Paper for Printed Library Materials, ANSI/NISO Z39.48-1992.

CONTENTS

PREFACE

What a difference a century makes.

In the recently completed 2018 season, an average of nearly sixteen million viewers tuned in each week to watch the National Football League (NFL). The league's championship game, the Super Bowl, now routinely draws more than a hundred million sets of eyeballs, and the day itself is akin to a national holiday. NFL players enjoy folk-hero status; we see them on television pitching insurance, bank cards, aftershave, soft drinks, computers, and just about everything else. Annual sales of licensed NFL products are in the billions. And the game is going global. Since 2007, the league has hosted games in London and Mexico City.

Considering the place of the modern NFL in American, and increasingly international, culture, it's difficult to imagine that the league has such modest origins. But when, nearly a century ago, the NFL was founded as the American Professional Football Association, the initial brainstorming session took place in Ralph Hay's Hupmobile Sales Agency in Canton, Ohio. In 1920, there were only fourteen teams, just four of which—the Chicago Cardinals, Chicago Tigers, Detroit Heralds, and Cleveland Tigers—were located in major cities. Other cities that had teams included Dayton, Akron, and Canton, in Ohio, and even smaller cities than those. Radio was the sole medium by which pro football fans could follow games in real time. If you didn't have a radio, then you had to wait until the next day's newspaper to learn the results of those games.

Today, the NFL fields thirty-two teams across the entire country. Green Bay, by far the smallest city with a team, has a population of little more than a hundred thousand. There are no teams in small towns like Hammond, Indiana, Muncie, Illinois, and Rochester, New York, like there used to be. In its first fifteen seasons, there wasn't even a set number of games for teams to play, but there was a minimum. NFL games are still broadcast on radio, but the main medium by which fans tune in these days is television. And, including the NFL Network, there are five channels that beam games across the land. All of the different camera angles that fans enjoy on TV these days could have only been dreamed of fifty to sixty years ago. Fans can still read about NFL games in newspapers, but with the Internet and smart phones, they don't have to wait until the next morning or afternoon to do it. With those two modes, fans get instantaneous news, not just about games but player statistics and feature stories, too. With fantasy football and betting on games, there is never too much information for fans in the twenty-first century.

The Baltimore Colts' 23–17 overtime win against the New York Giants on December 28, 1958, is widely regarded to be "The Greatest Game Ever Played." It was the first NFL postseason game to go into sudden-death overtime. Even though it was not the first NFL game to be televised, it marked the beginning of the NFL's popularity surge and eventual rise to the top of the U.S. sports market. A major reason was that the game was televised across the nation by NBC.

In the years to come, there were other memorable NFL postseason games that stand the test of time as classics. There was the "Ice Bowl" between Dallas and Green Bay on December 31, 1967. There was the double-overtime game between Miami and Kansas City on Christmas Day 1971, still the longest NFL game ever played. No one will forget the "Sea of Hands" contest between the Dolphins and Raiders on December 21, 1974. How about the famed San Diego–Miami game on January 2, 1982? Or the unforgettable Bills–Giants Super Bowl on January

27, 1991? More recently, there was the Patriots–Seahawks Super Bowl thriller on February 1, 2015.

The list is endless. The NFL is king. Attendance records are continually shattered. Even fans of the 0-16 Detroit Lions and 0-16 Cleveland Browns keep coming back for more. In honor of the 2019 season, the one hundredth NFL campaign, *A Century of NFL Football: The All-Time Quiz* gives readers a chance to relive memorable moments, games, and players' and coaches' achievements in quiz fashion chronologically. Statistics from the American Football League's 1960–1969 run are included since the NFL counts the AFL's stats in its official records. Not only are there hundreds of questions, but the substantial answers take readers on a unique ride through the league's rich history.

I hope you have fun along the way.

THE 1920s

BIRTH OF A NEW LEAGUE

In the early 1900s, aside from baseball, college football was king. There were a few professional leagues that were centered in Illinois, New York, Ohio, and Pennsylvania. In the late teens of the twentieth century, some leagues raided local colleges for players, but no draft existed. As a result, the leagues began to consolidate in order to gain control over their rosters and expenses. In 1920, the American Professional Football Association (APFA) was born, and the pro game became much more organized. Actually, the APFA was originally known as the American Professional Football Conference. Jim Thorpe, a former football and track star at the Carlisle Indian Industrial School in Pennsylvania and a double gold-medal winner at the 1912 Summer Olympics in Stockholm, Sweden, added credibility to the sport and was the APFA's first president. A membership fee of a hundred dollars per team was charged to give an appearance of respectability, but no team ever paid it. Scheduling was left up to the teams. And many of those teams came and went. Some of the great teams in the 1920s were the Canton Bulldogs, Frankford Yellow Jackets, and Providence Steam Roller. A few of the great players were Thorpe, Red Grange, and Ernie Nevers.

QUESTIONS

1. Where was the National Football League founded? *Answer on page 5.*

2. What team was the first champion of the American Professional Football Association? *Answer on page 5.*

3. What player with the initials G.T. was the American Professional Football Association's first all-pro center? *Answer on page 6.*

4. Helmets were mandatory for players in the 1920s. True or false? *Answer on page 6.*

5. What offensive formation was popular in the 1920s? *Answer on page 6.*

6. The Decatur Staleys became the Chicago Staleys in 1921 and the Chicago Bears in 1922. The first owner of the franchise was also its first head coach. Who was he? *Answer on page 7.*

7. Jim Thorpe played for six teams in his career, which lasted from 1920 through 1926 and 1928. Who was the first team for which he played? *Answer on page 8.*
   a. Detroit Heralds
   b. Rock Island Independents
   c. Canton Bulldogs
   d. Buffalo All-Americans

8. What team won back-to-back NFL Championships in 1922 and 1923? *Answer on page 9.*

9. The _____ Bulldogs won the 1924 NFL title. *Answer on page 10.*

10. In 1924, the Rochester Jeffersons finished in last place. What was their record? *Answer on page 11.*
    a. 0-3
    b. 0-5
    c. 0-7
    d. 0-9

11. I played halfback for seven seasons for the Chicago Bears and one season for the New York Yankees. My nickname was "The Galloping Ghost." Who am I? *Answer on page 11.*

12. The Chicago Cardinals won the 1925 NFL Championship. True or false? *Answer on page 12.*

13. What player who suited up for five teams from 1925 through 1938 with the initials J.B. was known for crazy, legendary exploits on and off the field? *Answer on page 14.*

14. The Los Angeles _____ played one season, 1926, and finished with a 6-3-1 record. *Answer on page 15.*

15. The Chicago Bears would have won the 1926 NFL Championship with a 12-1-3 record, a .923 winning percentage,

except for the fact that another team finished 14-1-2, a .933 winning percentage. What team was it? *Answer on page 15.*

16. Which New York team won the 1927 NFL Championship, the Giants or the Yankees? *Answer on page 16.*

17. What team won the 1928 NFL Championship? *Answer on page 17.*

   a. Green Bay Packers
   b. Providence Steam Roller
   c. Chicago Bears
   d. Detroit Wolverines

18. How many NFL titles did the Green Bay Packers of the 1920s win? *Answer on page 18.*

   a. One
   b. Two
   c. Three
   d. Four

19. What player with the initials E.N. set an NFL record that, although has been tied, still stands today—6 touchdowns in one game, on Thanksgiving 1929? *Answer on page 19.*

20. In 1929, Dayton finished in last place with an 0-6 record. What was the nickname of the team? *Answer on page 20.*

   a. Flyers
   b. Aztecs
   c. Triangles
   d. Bengals

ANSWERS

1. Canton, Ohio. Pro football actually began in 1892 in Pittsburgh when former Yale University star William "Pudge" Heffelfinger was paid five hundred dollars to play in a game for the Allegheny Athletic Association on November 12. For almost the next three decades, pro football faced its ups and downs as the game was played primarily in small towns throughout western Pennsylvania and the Midwest. The NFL was born on September 17, 1920, inside an automobile showroom in Canton. Representatives of eleven pro football teams gathered to create the American Professional Football Association (APFA). Two years later, the name was changed to the National Football League.

   Ralph E. Hay, a car dealer who had bought the Canton Bulldogs in 1918, met with the owners of the ten other teams—the Decatur Staleys, Chicago Cardinals, Akron Pros, Cleveland Indians, Dayton Triangles, Massillon Tigers, Hammond Pros, Muncie Flyers, Rock Island Independents, and Rochester Jeffersons. Hay realized that they all had to organize a league if pro football was going to survive. And so the APFA was born. By the time the APFA had its first season in 1920, there were fourteen teams.

2. The Akron Pros. The Pros originated as a semipro team called the Akron Indians. After experiencing financial losses from 1912 through 1919, the team in 1920 was sold to Art Ranney, an Akron businessman and former football player at the University of Akron, and Frank Nied, a cigar-store owner. Coached by Elgie Tobin, Akron finished with an 8-0-3 record and won the title based on that. There was no postseason in the APFA yet. The Pros outscored their opponents a combined 151–7. Those seven points they yielded came on November 14 in a 7–7 tie with the Cleveland Tigers, a team comprised mainly of ex-stars from the pro team the Massillon Tigers.

   Akron opened the season on October 3 with a 43–0 victory over the Wheeling Stogies. Al Nesser, one of the infamous football-playing "Nesser Brothers," scored three touchdowns on fumble recoveries. The next week, the Pros routed the Columbus Panhandles 37–0. Akron's first road game came on October 31, a 10–0 upset of the Canton Bulldogs, who were considered to be the top team in the APFA. On November 21, Akron, behind the rushing of Fritz Pollard and Frank McCormick, defeated the Dayton Triangles 13–0. The last two games of the season were scoreless ties with the Buffalo All-Americans and the Decatur Staleys, respectively.

3. George Trafton. Trafton played for the Decatur/Chicago Staleys in 1920 and 1921 and the Chicago Bears from 1923 through 1932. He played college football for one year at the University of Notre Dame. He was a member of Knute Rockne's 1919 Fighting Irish team that featured George Gipp. That year, the Irish finished 9-0 and were recognized as co–national champions by the National Championship Foundation. As a member of the Decatur Staleys in 1920, Trafton was selected as a first-team All-Pro. In 1921, he helped the Staleys to a 9-1-1 record and the APFA Championship. After taking a year off to become an assistant coach for Northwestern University, he returned to the Chicago team in 1923. He was an integral part of several successful Bears teams. In his final season, the Bears finished 7-1-6 in winning the NFL title. He was inducted into the Pro Football Hall of Fame in 1964.

4. True. Helmets, which were made of soft leather, were not worn by a lot of players. Most teams' uniforms looked the same as one another. From season to season, most teams changed what they wore. Most teams bought their uniforms used. Jerseys were usually made of a thick material, like wool.

5. The T formation. The T formation is a formation used in which three running backs line up in a row about 5 yards behind the quarterback, forming the shape of a T. The T formation is often said to be the oldest offensive formation in American football and is claimed to have been invented by Walter Camp in 1882. The T formation led to a faster-paced, higher-scoring game. However, as the forward pass was le-

galized, the original T formation became obsolete in favor of formations such as the single wing. Innovations, such as a smaller, more throwing-friendly ball, along with the invention of the hand-to-hand snap in the 1930s, led to the T formation's revival.

6. George Halas. "Papa Bear" Halas was the owner of the Bears until his death on October 31, 1983. He was the Bears' head coach from 1920 through 1929, 1933 through 1942, and 1946 through 1967. He wore a third hat, too, as a wide receiver and defensive end for the team from 1920 through 1928.

Halas played football for the University of Illinois. He also played baseball and basketball there. He helped the Fighting Illini win the 1918 Western Conference (now Big Ten Conference) football title. He was named Most Valuable Player of the 1919 Rose Bowl as a member of the Great Lakes Naval Training Station team. In that game, he caught a touchdown pass and returned an interception 77 yards. Halas actually played twelve games as an outfielder for the New York Yankees in 1919, but a hip injury ended his baseball career.

Although he led the Decatur Staleys to a 10-1-2 record in 1920, the franchise suffered financial losses, prompting Halas to move the team to Chicago. In 1921, the Staleys won the APFA Championship with a 9-1-1 record. In 1922, the team's nickname was changed to "Bears." Halas led the Bears to winning records, including a 12-1-3 mark in 1926, until 1929, when the team finished 4-9-2. After stepping away for three years, Halas made a triumphant return as the Bears' head coach in 1933 by leading them to a 10-2-1 record, the championship of the Western Division, and a 23–21 victory over the New York Giants in the NFL title game. The next year, Chicago won all thirteen of its regular-season games but failed in its bid to repeat as champion by falling to the same Giants 30–13 in the league title game.

During the next eight seasons, Halas and the Bears posted winning records, including NFL Championships in 1940 and

1941. In 1942, Halas led the Bears to a 5-0 record but had to leave the team at that point to fight in World War II as a member of the navy. He returned to the team in 1946 and led them to an 8-2-1 record and another NFL title. The Bears continued to have successful seasons, for the most part, all the way through 1963, when Halas led the team to its last NFL Championship with him as head coach. After Halas retired from coaching, the Bears fell on hard times until a couple of playoff berths in the late 1970s. Halas was inducted into the charter class of the Pro Football Hall of Fame in 1963.

7. c. Canton Bulldogs. Thorpe played for, and was the head coach of, the Bulldogs in 1920. He helped them to a 7-4-2 record. He was also the first president of the American Professional Football Association in 1920. Before that, he became the first Native American to win a gold medal for the United States. Considered to be one of the most versatile athletes in modern sports, he won Summer Olympic gold medals in the 1912 pentathlon and decathlon. He also played professional baseball and basketball. Football was his best sport, however. He was a two-time All-American as a member of the Carlisle Indian Industrial School, the college football team for which he played. As a running back, defensive back, placekicker, and punter in 1911, he kicked 4 field goals in helping the Indians to an 18–15 upset of Harvard. The next year, Carlisle won the national collegiate championship due in large part to Thorpe's 1,869 rushing yards, 27 touchdowns, and 224 points. In a win over Army that year, he scored on a 97-yard touchdown run and was named All-American for the second straight season.

Thorpe was the player-coach for the football Cleveland Indians in 1921 and for the Oorang Indians in 1922 and 1923. After that, his focus was solely on playing. Other teams he played for in his career were the Rock Island Independents, the New York Giants, and the Chicago Cardinals.

Thorpe was inducted into the Pro Football Hall of Fame's inaugural class of 1963.

Jim Thorpe
Harris & Ewing/Library of Congress

8. The Canton Bulldogs. Led by players such as Guy Chamberlain (7 touchdowns), Ed Shaw (4 touchdowns, 2 field goals), Norb Sacksteder (4 touchdowns), Harry Robb (3 touchdowns), and Pete Henry (2 field goals), Canton finished 10-0-2 in 1922. The Bulldogs outscored their opponents a combined 184–15. They began the season by routing the Louisville Brecks 38–0 on October 1. After a scoreless tie with the Dayton Triangles, they beat the Oorang Indians and the Akron Pros 14–0 and 22–0, respectively. They concluded the season by whipping the Milwaukee Badgers 40–6 and then the Toledo Maroons 19–0.

Led by Henry (1 touchdown, 9 field goals), Lou Smyth (7 touchdowns), Doc Elliott (6 touchdowns), Ben Jones (6 touchdowns), and Tex Grigg (4 touchdowns), the 1923 Bulldogs finished 11-0-1, the tie coming against the Buffalo All-Americans by a 3–3 score on November 11. They outscored their opponents a combined 246–19. They opened the season with shutouts of the Hammond Pros (17–0), Louisville (37–0), Dayton (30–0), and the Chicago Bears (6–0). They ended the season with shutouts of Toledo Maroons (28–0), Buffalo (14–0), and the Columbus Tigers (10–0).

9. Cleveland. The Bulldogs finished 7-1-1 and outscored its opponents 229–60. Scoring leaders were Doc Elliott and Dave Noble with 6 touchdowns apiece; Ben Jones, Link Lyman, and Wooky Roberts with 4 touchdowns each; and Hoge Workman with 3 field goals. The Bulldogs began the season by beating the Chicago Bears 16–14 on October 5 at Dunn Field in Cleveland. In that game, the home team took a 3–0 lead on a 20-yard field goal by Elliott. Chicago took a 7–3 lead after one quarter on a touchdown pass from Laurie Walquist to Joey Sternaman. Jones scored on a touchdown run in the third quarter as Cleveland forged back ahead 10–7. Later in the quarter, Olin Smith recovered a blocked punt in the Chicago end zone for a 16–7 Bulldogs' lead. Sternaman returned a punt 70 yards for a touchdown in the fourth quarter for the game's final points.

After a 3–3 tie with the Frankford Yellow Jackets, Cleveland beat the Akron Pros 29–14, the Rochester Jeffersons 59–0, and the Dayton Triangles 35–0 before defeating Akron again 20–7 on November 9. A week later, on November 16, came the Bulldogs' only loss of the season, 12–7 at home against Frankford. In that game, Jim Welsh kicked a field goal in both the first and second quarters to give the Yellow Jackets a 6–0 halftime lead. Tex Hamer's touchdown run in the third quarter upped the Frankford lead to 12–0. Noble scored on a touchdown run in the fourth quarter for the game's final points. The next week, the Bulldogs beat the Columbus Tigers 7–0, and four days later in the season finale on Thanksgiving, with the help of 4 touchdown runs by Elliott, they routed the visiting Milwaukee Badgers 53–10.

10. c. 0-7. Rochester was outscored by its opponents 156–7. The Jeffersons began the season with a 21–0 loss at Frankford on September 27. The Yellow Jackets took a 7–0 first-quarter lead when Tex Hamer completed a 32-yard touchdown pass to Eddie Doyle. The score stayed the same until the fourth quarter when Jack Storer scored on a 5-yard run to make it 14–0. Jack Finn rushed for a 3-yard touchdown for the game's final points.

The next week, Rochester lost at home 3–0 to the Akron Pros. On October 12, also at home, they fell 15–7 to the Columbus Tigers, the only game all season in which they were able to score. In that game, Columbus scored a safety in the first quarter for a 2–0 lead. In the second quarter, Sonny Winters threw a touchdown pass to Bob Rapp to make the score 8–0. Winters and Rapp hooked up again in the third quarter to increase the Tigers' lead to 15–0. In the fourth quarter, Rochester scored the game's final points on a touchdown run by Jerry Noonan. The Jeffersons lost their last four games of the season to the Buffalo Bisons (26–0), the Cleveland Bulldogs (59–0), Columbus (16–0), and Buffalo again (16–0).

11. Red Grange. I played for the University of Illinois from 1923 through 1925. In my first collegiate game on October 6, 1923, as a sophomore, I scored 3 touchdowns in a 24–7 victory over Nebraska. In seven games that season, I rushed for 726 yards and scored 12 touchdowns in leading the Fighting Illini to an 8-0 record, the Western Conference (now Big Ten Conference) title, and the Helms Athletic Foundation National Championship. As a junior, I ran for 743 yards, passed for 433 yards, scored 13 touchdowns, and had 4 interceptions in helping Illinois to a 6-1-1 record. In my senior year of 1925, I rushed for 605 yards, scored 6

touchdowns, and had 7 interceptions in leading the Illini to a 5-3 record. I once scored 4 touchdowns in twelve minutes in college.

I signed with the Bears the day after my last collegiate game. I played with them for the last five games of the 1925 season. On December 6 that year, some seventy thousand fans showed up at the Polo Grounds in New York to watch me help save the Giants franchise. I returned an interception 35 yards for a touchdown as we won 19–7. In the five games, I gained more than 400 total yards and scored 3 touchdowns.

I had a dispute with the Bears and left to form my own league, the American Football League. It lasted only one season, after which my team, the New York Yankees, was merged into the NFL. In 1927, during my one NFL season with the Yankees, I suffered a serious knee injury against Chicago. After sitting out 1928, I returned to the Bears. In 1932, I rushed for 136 yards with 3 touchdowns and had 11 receptions for 168 yards with 4 touchdowns in helping us to the NFL Championship. In 1933, I rushed for 277 yards with a touchdown and passed for 169 yards with 2 touchdowns in leading us to a 10-2-1 record and the Western Division title. We beat the Giants 23–21 in the championship game at Wrigley Field, a game in which I made a touchdown-saving tackle that saved the game for us. In 1934, I rushed for 156 yards and a touchdown in helping us to a 13-0 record, but we lost to the Giants in the NFL title game.

I was inducted into the Pro Football Hall of Fame's charter class of 1963.

12. True. The Cardinals finished 11-2-1 and outscored their opponents 230–65. Their only road game of the entire season was a scoreless tie with the Chicago Bears on Thanksgiving. The Cardinals began the season on September 27 with a 10–6 home loss to the Hammond Pros. Seven days later, on October 4, they routed the Milwaukee Badgers

Chicago Bears teammates practicing as Joe Zeller tries to tackle Red Grange
Alan Fisher, World Telegram & Sun/*Library of Congress*

34–0. In that game, Red Dunn scored on two runs in the second quarter to give Chicago a 14–0 halftime lead. Dunn threw a touchdown pass to Hal Erickson to up the Cardinals' lead to 21–0 after three quarters. In the fourth quarter, Paddy Driscoll sandwiched 2 field goals around his own touchdown run. During the next five weeks, the Cards beat the Columbus Tigers, the Kansas City Cowboys, the Bears, the Duluth Kelleys, and the Green Bay Packers to improve their record to 6-1.

Next came a 23–6 triumph over the Buffalo Bisons on November 15. In that game, after the Cardinals scored on a first-quarter safety, they increased their lead to 9–0 on a 4-yard touchdown run by Driscoll. Buffalo cut it to 9–6 after one quarter when Jim Kendrick scored from a yard out. Erickson ran for a touchdown in the second quarter to expand the Chicago lead to 16–6, and Bob Koehler's 4-yard touchdown run in the fourth quarter accounted for the game's final points. The Cardinals shut out both the Dayton Triangles 14–0 the next week and the Rock Island Independents 7–0 on November 29 before falling to the Pottsville Maroons 21–7 a week later. They concluded the season with shutouts of Milwaukee (59–0) and Hammond (13–0).

Overall, Erickson led the way for Chicago with 7 touchdowns. Driscoll, Koehler, and Art Folz each scored 4 touchdowns. Driscoll also kicked 11 field goals. Dunn scored 3 touchdowns.

13. Johnny Blood. Blood, whose given last name was McNally, played several offensive positions for the Milwaukee Badgers, Duluth Eskimos, Pottsville Maroons, Green Bay Packers, and Pittsburgh Pirates (now Pittsburgh Steelers). He scored a total of 42 touchdowns, 37 of them receiving, with a high of 11 receiving touchdowns as a member of the 1931 NFL champion Packers. He was enshrined into the inaugural class of the Pro Football Hall of Fame in 1963.

As for his outrageous stunts, the following is a sampling of some of the things he did:

* Leaped across a narrow ledge six stories high to get into a hotel room in Los Angeles
* Played nearly an entire game with a collapsed kidney
* Was rescued by teammates while trying chin-ups on the stern's flagpole of the SS *Mariposa* while traveling across the Pacific Ocean for a barnstorming game in Hawaii
* Rode the blinds between trains on the way to training camp to evade having to pay a fare, which earned him the nickname "The Vagabond Halfback"
* Raced 50 yards for a touchdown on a lateral from quarterback Red Dunn. When Dunn called the same play later in the game, Blood simply smiled and lateraled the ball back to him.
* Climbed down the face of a hotel in downtown Chicago to avoid curfew and perform poetry to swooning women below

* Was acclaimed for perching on hotel ledges and the tops
  of bar tables as he chanted the song "Galway Bay"
* Turned down an opportunity to buy an NFL franchise
  for $1,200

14. Buccaneers. All ten of the Buccaneers' games were on the
    road. They began the season by losing 15–0 to the Chicago
    Cardinals on September 26. A week later, they beat the Mil-
    waukee Badgers 6–0. Their third game was on October 17,
    a 16–13 victory over the Canton Bulldogs. In that game,
    Canton took a 7–0 second-quarter lead when Cliff Marker
    recovered a fumble in the Los Angeles end zone. The Buc-
    caneers cut their deficit to 7–6 at halftime on a thirty-yard
    touchdown pass from Tuffy Maul to Tut Imlay. In the third
    quarter, the Bulldogs upped their lead to 13–6 when Harry
    Robb rushed for a touchdown. Later in the quarter, Maul
    ran for a 1-yard touchdown as Los Angeles tied the score
    13–13. Maul's 17-yard field goal in the fourth quarter was
    the game's final points.

    The next Sunday, the Bucs played to a scoreless tie with
    the Buffalo Rangers. In their following three games, they
    beat the Providence Steam Roller, lost to the Pottsville Ma-
    roons, and beat the New York Giants. Then, on November
    21, they defeated the Brooklyn Lions 20–0 at Ebbets Field.
    In that game, Los Angeles took a 7–0 halftime lead on a 15-
    yard touchdown run by Imlay in the second quarter. Imlay
    scored on a short touchdown run in the third quarter to in-
    crease the Buccaneers' lead to 14–0. Later in the third, Don
    Thompson returned a fumble 20 yards for a touchdown and
    the game's final points.

    Overall for Los Angeles, Imlay scored 4 touchdowns.
    Maul and Thompson both scored 2 touchdowns. Maul also
    kicked 2 field goals.

15. Frankford Yellow Jackets. After opening the season by play-
    ing to a 6–6 tie with the Akron Indians on September 25,
    Frankford posted six straight shutouts, the last of which
    was 17–0 over the Canton Bulldogs on October 23. In

that game, after a scoreless first half, Max Reed recovered a blocked punt in the Canton end zone to give Frankford a 7–0 lead after three quarters. In the fourth quarter, Hap Moran scored on a 38-yard run to make it 14–0. Johnny Budd kicked a 22-yard field goal for the game's final points.

Next came a strange bit of scheduling. On October 30, the Yellow Jackets lost 7–6 at home to the Providence Steam Roller, then came back the very next day, on October 31, to beat the same Providence team 6–3 on the road. Frankford then won seven straight games, the last of which was 24–0 at home against the Steam Roller. In that game, fullback Hust Stockton gave the Yellow Jackets a 7–0 first-quarter lead on a touchdown run. Ed Weir's 20-yard field goal in the second quarter made it 10–0 at the half. Swede Youngstrom recovered a blocked punt in the end zone for a 17–0 lead after three quarters. The game's final points came in the fourth quarter on a rushing touchdown by Two-Bits Homan. The last game of the season was a scoreless tie with the Pottsville Maroons.

Overall for Frankford, Ben Jones scored 9 touchdowns. Moran scored 5 touchdowns. With 3 touchdowns apiece were Homan, Doc Bruder, and Ned Wilcox. Budd kicked 6 field goals.

16. The Giants. The Giants easily won the title with a record of 11-1-1, outscoring their opponents 197–20. They began the season with an 8–0 victory over the Steam Roller at Providence on September 25. A scoreless tie with the Cleveland Bulldogs was followed by a 19–0 win over the Pottsville Maroons and a 6–0 loss to Cleveland. The Giants shut out their next five opponents—the Frankford Yellow Jackets (13–0 and 27–0), Pottsville (16–0), the Duluth Eskimos (21–0), and Providence (25–0). In the win over the visiting Steam Roller on Tuesday—yes, Tuesday—November 8 at the Polo Grounds, New York jumped out to a 7–0 first-quarter lead on a 54-yard interception return by Mule Wilson. In the second quarter, Jack Hagerty caught a

39-yard touchdown pass from Jack McBride to increase the Giants' lead to 13–0 at halftime. Hagerty returned a punt 53 yards for a touchdown in the third quarter to make the score 19–0. The final points of the game came on a 9-yard touchdown pass from McBride to Hinkey Haines.

Two weeks later, on November 20, New York beat the visiting Chicago Cardinals 28–7. The Giants took a 21–0 lead after one quarter. First, McBride threw a 12-yard touchdown pass to Haines for a 7–0 lead. Then McBride scored a touchdown on a 10-yard run. After that, Wilson caught a 25-yard touchdown pass from McBride. Chicago got on the board in the third quarter on a 2-yard touchdown pass from Evar Swanson to John Vesser to make it 21–7. Doug Wycoff's short touchdown run in the fourth quarter was the game's final points. The Giants closed out the season with a win over the Chicago Bears and two shutouts of the New York Yankees.

Overall for New York, McBride, Haines, and Wilson each scored 6 touchdowns. McBride also kicked 2 field goals. Wycoff, Hagerty, and Phil White each scored 3 touchdowns.

17. b. Providence Steam Roller. Providence finished 8-1-2, outscoring its opponents 128–42. The Steam Roller opened the season on September 30 with a 20–7 home win over the New York Yankees. Providence took a 7–0 first-quarter lead when Pop Williams scored on a 2-yard touchdown run. New York tied the score later in the first on a 62-yard interception return by Gibby Welch. In the second quarter, Williams scored on a 10-yard touchdown run to give the Steam Roller the lead again, 14–7. Later in the quarter, Curly Oden ran one in from 4 yards out for the game's final points.

After falling to Frankford 10–6, Providence beat the Dayton Triangles, the Yankees, the Pottsville Maroons, and Detroit to improve to 5-1. Then came a 6–6 tie with the Frankford Yellow Jackets on November 17. The Steam Roller then beat Frankford the very next day before shutting out the New York Giants 16–0 at home on November 25.

In that game, Jack Cronin opened the scoring with a 2-yard touchdown run in the second quarter to give Providence a 6–0 lead. Gus Sonnenberg's 28-yard field goal made it 9–0 at halftime. In the fourth quarter, Cronin scored from a yard out for the game's final points. The Steam Roller closed the season with a 7–0 win over the Pottsville Maroons and a 7–7 tie with the Packers.

Overall for Providence, Wildcat Wilson scored 5 touchdowns. Williams and Oden each scored 4 touchdowns, while Cronin scored 3 touchdowns.

18. a. One. Under player-coach Curly Lambeau, the Packers had all winning records in the 1920s, but they saved their best season of the decade for last—they finished 12-0-1 in 1929 and won the NFL Championship. They outscored their opponents 198–22. After opening the season on September 22 by beating the Dayton Triangles 9–0 at home, the Packers hosted the rival Chicago Bears a week later. After a scoreless first quarter, Herdis McCrary rushed for a touchdown to give Green Bay a 7–0 second-quarter lead. Tom Nash threw a 15-yard touchdown pass to Johnny Blood to increase the lead to 14–0 at halftime. In the third quarter, the Packers scored a safety when a punt they blocked rolled out of the Chicago end zone. Later in the quarter, Bo Molenda scored on a 10-yard touchdown run for the final points in a 23–0 Packers victory.

During the next five weeks, Green Bay beat the Chicago Cardinals, Frankford Yellow Jackets, Minneapolis Red Jackets, and then both the Cardinals and Red Jackets again before a rematch with the Bears at Wrigley Field in Chicago on November 10. McCrary scored both of Green Bay's touchdowns in a 14–0 triumph—on a reception and an interception in the end zone. The Packers won three of their next four games, which included a scoreless tie with the Yellow Jackets at Frankford on Thanksgiving. They concluded the season with a third win over the Bears, 25–0, again at Wrigley Field, on December 8. Cully Lidberg gave the visitors a 6–0 first-quarter lead on a rushing touchdown. Verne Lewellen did the same thing in the third quarter for a 12–0 advantage. Later in the third, Eddie Kotal caught touchdown catches from Red Dunn and Lewellen, respectively, for the game's final points.

Overall for Green Bay, Lewellen scored 8 touchdowns. Blood scored 5 touchdowns, while McCrary scored 4. Tallying 3 touchdowns apiece were Molenda, Kotal, and Lavvie Dilweg. Dunn kicked 2 field goals.

19. Ernie Nevers. Nevers, a fullback, accomplished the feat as a member of the Chicago Cardinals in a 40–6 thumping of the Bears at Wrigley Field. He played his college ball at Stanford University. In the final game of his sophomore season in 1923 against California, he gained more yards than the entire Golden Bears team! After missing most of his junior year due to two broken ankles, he helped the Cardinals to a 7-2 record and was a consensus All-American his senior year.

After giving Major League Baseball a try with a brief stint as a pitcher for the St. Louis Browns in 1926 (he would try again in 1927 and 1928), that same year Nevers joined the Duluth Eskimos of the NFL. He played for Duluth in 1926 and 1927. In 1926, he scored 8 touchdowns and kicked 4 field goals. The next season, he scored 4 touchdowns. After sitting out the 1928 season, Nevers joined the Cardinals in 1929. That year, he scored 12 touchdowns and kicked a field goal. Six of the touchdowns came in that Thanksgiving game against the Bears. All six of Nevers's touchdowns came on rushes—2 in the first quarter, 1 in the second quarter, 1 in the third quarter, and 2 in the fourth quarter. The Bears' only score came in the third quarter on a 60-yard touchdown pass from Walt Holmer to Gardie Grange, Red Grange's younger brother.

The next year, in 1930, Nevers scored 6 touchdowns and kicked a field goal, and in 1931 he scored 8 touchdowns and kicked a field goal. He doubled as the Cardinals' head coach both seasons. He was inducted into the Pro Football Hall of Fame's charter class of 1963.

20. c. Triangles. The Triangles were outscored by their opponents 136–7. All of their games were on the road. They began the season on September 22 with a 9–0 loss to the Green Bay Packers. Six days later, they lost 14–7 to the Frankford Yellow Jackets, the only game all season in which they scored points. Frankford took a 7–0 first-quarter lead when Wally Diehl scored on a 6-yard run. In the second quarter, a 30-yard touchdown pass from Wild Bill Kelly to Ed Halicki upped the lead to 14–0. Dayton cut its deficit to 14–7 in the third quarter on a 30-yard fumble return for a touchdown by Al Graham. That turned out to be the final points of the game.

The next day, the Triangles lost 41–0 to the Providence Steam Roller. A week later, they fell 12–0 to the Staten Island Stapletons. Then came a 41–0 beating at the hands of the Boston Bulldogs. The season finale was a month and a half later, believe it or not, a 19–0 loss to the Chicago Cardinals on November 24. In that game, Ernie Nevers scored each of Chicago's 3 touchdowns—a 3-yard run in the first quarter, another 3-yard run in the second quarter, and a 1-yard run in the third quarter.

THE 1930s

EXPANSION TO BIG CITIES

In the first few years of the 1930s, many of the NFL teams were still from smaller cities. But, by 1933, the league said "sayonara" to those smaller towns and expanded into more, bigger cities such as Boston, Philadelphia, Pittsburgh, and Cincinnati. Another change in 1933 was the advent of divisional play, with an Eastern Division and a Western Division of five teams each, with the champions of each playing one another in the NFL Championship game.

QUESTIONS

1. What team finished with a record of 1-10-1 and in last place in 1930? *Answer on page 24.*

   a. Frankford Yellow Jackets
   b. Newark Tornadoes
   c. Chicago Bears
   d. Chicago Cardinals

2. What team won back-to-back NFL Championships in 1930 and 1931? *Answer on page 25.*

3. It became mandatory for NFL players to wear helmets in the 1930s. True or false? *Answer on page 26.*

4. What happened at the end of the 1932 season that brought divisional play for the first time in 1933? *Answer on page 26.*

5. What major rule change was made regarding the passing game in 1933? *Answer on page 26.*

6. I was the founding owner of the Pittsburgh Steelers. Who am I? *Answer on page 27.*

7. What two teams opposed one another in the 1933 NFL Championship game? *Answer on page 27.*

8. In 1934, the Chicago Bears finished 13-0 and won the NFL Championship. True or false? *Answer on page 28.*

9. In what year did the Portsmouth Spartans become the Detroit Lions? *Answer on page 29.*

   a. 1933
   b. 1934
   c. 1935
   d. 1936

10. Who, with the initials B.F., was the first NFL player to rush for a thousand yards in a season? *Answer on page 29.*

11. What unique feat did the 1935 Chicago Bears and Chicago Cardinals achieve? *Answer on page 29.*

12. The _____ won their first NFL title in 1935. *Answer on page 31.*

13. What was the first season in which all NFL teams played the same number of games? *Answer on page 33.*

    a. 1934
    b. 1935
    c. 1936
    d. 1937

14. The 1936 Green Bay Packers finished 10-1-1 and won the NFL Championship. To what team did the Packers lose their only game? *Answer on page 34.*

    a. Detroit Lions
    b. Philadelphia Eagles
    c. Brooklyn Dodgers
    d. Chicago Bears

15. To what city did the Boston Redskins relocate in 1937? *Answer on page 35.*

16. What was the nickname of the expansion Cleveland team in 1937? *Answer on page 36.*

17. Byron "Whizzer" White was the Associate Justice of the Supreme Court of the United States from 1962 through 1993. He played for three years in the NFL. For what two teams did he play? *Answer on page 38.*

18. In 1938, the Eastern Division Championship came down to the final Sunday between what two teams head-to-head? *Answer on page 39.*

   a. New York Giants, Philadelphia Eagles
   b. Brooklyn Dodgers, Washington Redskins
   c. Philadelphia Eagles, Chicago Bears
   d. New York Giants, Washington Redskins

19. What team won the 1939 NFL Championship? *Answer on page 40.*

20. Name the two fullbacks who were on the NFL 1930s All-Decade Team. *Answer on page 41.*

ANSWERS

1. b. Newark Tornadoes. The Tornadoes lost their first four games, including one by 32–0 to the New York Giants on September 17. Ossie Wiberg gave New York a 7–0 first-quarter lead when he rushed for a touchdown. The lead grew to 13–0 at halftime on a 10-yard touchdown run by Len Sedbrook in the second quarter. In the third quarter, Sedbrook caught a 15-yard touchdown pass from Red Badgro to make it 19–0. Later in the third, Benny Friedman threw a 10-yard touchdown pass to Dosey Hoard for a 26–0 Giants lead. Friedman scored on a 10-yard run in the fourth quarter for the game's final points.

   After tying the Staten Island Stapletons 7–7 on October 1, Newark recorded its only victory of the season three days later, 19–0 on the road over the Frankford Yellow Jackets. In that game, the Tornadoes took a 6–0 first-quarter lead when Bud Ellor recovered a blocked punt in the end zone. Later in the quarter, Tom Leary returned an interception 55 yards for a touchdown to increase the lead to 12–0. Leary did it again in the second quarter, returning an interception 80 yards for a touchdown for the game's final points. Newark got shut out in their next five games and ended the season with a 34–7 loss to the Giants.

2. The Green Bay Packers. The Packers finished 10-3-1 in 1930, edging out the New York Giants by four percentage points. They outscored their opponents 234–111. They won their first eight games, including a 47–13 rout of the Portsmouth Spartans at home on November 2. In that game, Verne Lewellen scored on short touchdown runs in both the first and second quarters to give Green Bay a 14–0 lead. Bo Molenda's 1-yard touchdown run later in the second quarter upped the Packers' lead to 20–0 at halftime. In the third quarter, Herdis McCrary caught 42- and 27-yard touchdown passes from Red Dunn as the home team upped its lead to 33–6 after three quarters. In the fourth quarter, Paul Fitzgibbon scored on a short touchdown run, and Lewellen completed a 3-yard touchdown pass to Lavvie Dilweg for the game's final points. The Packers were powered by two late-November road wins, 25–7 over the Frankford Yellow Jackets on Thanksgiving and 37–7 over the Staten Island Stapletons three days later.

Overall for Green Bay in 1930, Lewellen scored 9 touchdowns, McCrary scored 6 touchdowns, and Johnny Blood had 5 touchdowns.

The 1931 Packers finished 12-2, a game ahead of the 11-3 Spartans, outscoring their opponents 291–87. They won their first nine games, including a 48–20 rout of the Providence Steam Roller on October 25 at home. In that game, the Packers jumped out to a 21–0 lead after one quarter on three Wuert Engelmann touchdowns. The first two were touchdown passes from Dunn, and the third was an 85-yard kickoff return. By halftime, the Green Bay lead was 28–7, but after three quarters, the Steam Roller closed the gap to 28–20. The Packers scored 3 touchdowns in the fourth quarter

—on a 45-yard run by Mule Wilson, a 4-yard run by Molenda, and a 40-yard pass from Molenda to Roger Grove.

Overall for Green Bay in 1931, Blood scored 14 touchdowns, and Lewellen scored 6 touchdowns.

3. True. Hard leather was what they were made of. Also, jerseys were still made of thick material. They were typically in basic colors. For identification purposes, numbers were put on jerseys by many teams.

4. The season ended with the Chicago Bears (6-1-6) and the Portsmouth Spartans (6-1-4) tied for first in the league standings. At the time, teams were ranked on a single table, and the team with the highest winning percentage (not including ties, which were not counted in the standings) at the end of the season was declared the champion. The only tiebreaker was that if two teams played twice in a season the result of the second game determined the title. This method had been used since the league's creation in 1920, but no situation had been encountered where two teams were tied for first. On top of that, the two games played in 1932 between Chicago and Portsmouth ended in ties.

The NFL quickly determined that a playoff game between the Bears and Spartans was needed to decide its champion. The teams were originally scheduled to stage the playoff game, officially a regular-season game that would count toward the regular-season standings, at Wrigley Field in Chicago on December 18. But a combination of heavy snow and extreme cold forced the game to be moved indoors to Chicago Stadium, which did not have a regulation-size football field. Playing with altered rules to accommodate the smaller playing field, the Bears won the game 9–0 and thus won the championship. Fan interest in the de facto championship game led the NFL, beginning the next year, to split into two divisions with a championship game to be played between the division titlists.

5. Quarterbacks were permitted to pass the ball from anywhere behind the line of scrimmage after having been allowed to throw it only when they were at least 5 yards behind the line

of scrimmage. The new rule stemmed from a controversial play that occurred during a 1932 game between the Chicago Bears and Portsmouth Spartans, a contest that was, for all intents and purposes, for the NFL Championship. With the game scoreless in the fourth quarter, the Bears' Bronko Nagurski faked a run toward the line of scrimmage and then quickly threw a 2-yard touchdown pass to Red Grange to give Chicago a 7–0 lead. Portsmouth contested that Nagurski was not 5 yards behind the line of scrimmage when he passed the ball. The play stood, and the Bears later added a safety to put the 9–0 victory on ice. At the NFL meetings the next off-season, Spartans head coach Potsy Clark requested that a change be made in the rules to allow passes anywhere behind the line of scrimmage, and the rule was changed to allow it.

6. Art Rooney. Known as "The Chief," I was also the first president of the Steelers from 1933 through 1974 and the first chairman of the team from 1933 until my death on August 25, 1988. I named the new team the "Pirates," which was also the name of the city's long-established Major League Baseball team of which I was a fan since childhood. Since the NFL's inception in 1920, the league had wanted a team in Pittsburgh due to the city's already long history with football, including the popularity of the University of Pittsburgh Panthers football team, an NCAA national championship contender during this period. The NFL was finally able to take advantage of Pennsylvania relaxing their blue laws that, prior to 1933, prohibited sporting events from taking place on Sundays, when most NFL games take place. We had losing seasons in six of our first seven seasons, from 1933 through 1939, and for the most part were an average-at-best franchise until the early 1970s when things drastically improved.

I was inducted into the Pro Football Hall of Fame in 1964.

7. The New York Giants and Chicago Bears. The Giants won the Eastern Division with a record of 11-3, while the Bears won the Western Division with a record of 10-2-1. They were, by far, the only two teams to finish in double figures in wins.

The Giants split their first four games of the season before routing the Philadelphia Eagles 56–0 on October 15 at the Polo Grounds in New York. They beat the Brooklyn Dodgers 21–7 the next week before falling to the Bears 14–10 on October 29 at Wrigley Field. The Giants won their last seven games of the season. The Bears won their first six games on the schedule before losing to the Boston Redskins 10–0 on November 5. The next week, they tied the Eagles 3–3, then seven days later lost 3–0 to the Giants. The Bears won their last four games of the season.

The championship game, played on December 17 at Wrigley Field, was a back-and-forth, exciting game. The Bears took a 3–0 lead after one quarter on a 16-yard field goal by Jack Manders. Manders made it 6–0 in the second quarter when he kicked a 40-yard field goal. The Giants took a 7–6 halftime lead when Red Badgro caught a 29-yard touchdown pass from Harry Newman. In the third quarter, Manders made good on a 28-yard field goal as Chicago forged back ahead 9–7. Later in the third, Max Krause scored on a 1-yard touchdown run to put New York back in the lead, 14–9. The Bears took back the lead 16–14 after three quarters on an 8-yard touchdown pass from Bronko Nagurski to Bill Carr. In the fourth quarter, the Giants went back ahead 21–16 when Newman hit Ken Strong on an 8-yard touchdown pass. Later in the quarter, Karr took a lateral and ran 19 yards for a touchdown for the winning points in a 23–21 Chicago victory.

8. False. The Bears did finish 13-0, but they lost to the New York Giants 30–13 in the NFL title game. They outscored their opponents 286–86. They opened the season with a 24–10 win over the Packers on September 23 at City Stadium in Green Bay. Jack Manders kicked a 24-yard field goal to give Chicago a 3–0 first-quarter lead. The Packers tied the score in the second quarter on a 16-yard field goal by Bob Monnett. In the third quarter, the Bears took a 10–3 lead when Bill Hewitt caught a 7-yard touchdown pass from Bronko Nagurski. The Packers tied the game 10–10 later in the quarter

on an 11-yard touchdown run by Buckets Goldenberg. In the fourth quarter, Nagurski scored on runs of 1 yard and 40 yards for the final points of the game.

During the next five weeks, the Bears beat the Cincinnati Reds, Brooklyn Dodgers, Pittsburgh Pirates, Chicago Cardinals, and Cincinnati again to improve to 6-0. Next came a rematch with Green Bay on October 28 at Wrigley Field. The Bears took a 7–0 first-quarter lead on an 18-yard touchdown pass from Gene Ronzani to Beattie Feathers. The Packers tied the game in the second quarter when Monnett completed a 9-yard touchdown pass to Al Rose. Manders knocked home an 18-yard field goal to give Chicago a 10–7 lead at halftime. In the third quarter, Ronzani threw a 27-yard touchdown pass to Carl Brumbaugh to up the Bears' lead to 17–7. In the fourth quarter, Manders booted a 28-yard field goal to make the score 20–7. Green Bay cut its deficit to 20–14 when Lavvie Dilweg caught a 13-yard touchdown pass from Arnie Herber. Feathers scored on a 46-yard run to give the Bears a 27–14 triumph.

Overall in 1934, Feathers had 119 rushes for 1,004 yards with 8 touchdowns and had 6 receptions for 174 yards. Nagurski ran the ball 123 times for 586 yards with 7 touchdowns, while Ronzani had 84 carries for 485 yards. Ronzani also had 5 receptions for 114 yards with 3 touchdowns. Hewitt had 11 catches for 151 yards with 5 touchdowns.

9. b. 1934. The Lions improved to 10-3 after a 6-5 record the year before. They outscored their opponents 238–59. They began the season by blanking their first seven opponents, the last of which was a 38–0 trouncing of the Cincinnati Reds on October 28. In that game, Dutch Clark gave Detroit a 3–0 first-quarter lead on a 25-yard field goal. In the second quarter, Glenn Presnell had a 6-yard touchdown run and kicked a 22-yard field goal for a 13–0 Lions lead at halftime. In the third quarter, Clark scored on runs of 82 yards and 1 yard to up the Lions' lead to 25–0. By the end of the third quarter, the score was 32–0, and the Lions put it in cruise control the

rest of the way. Detroit won its next three games against the Pittsburgh Pirates (40–7), the Chicago Cardinals (17–13), and the St. Louis Gunners (40–7) to improve to 10-0. They lost their last three games to the Green Bay Packers and twice to the Chicago Bears.

Overall in 1934, Presnell was 13-of-57 for 223 yards with 2 touchdowns and 8 interceptions. He rushed the ball 108 times for 413 yards with 7 touchdowns. Clark was 23-of-50 for 383 yards. He ran the ball 123 times for 763 yards with 8 touchdowns and had 6 receptions for 72 yards. Harry Ebding had 10 receptions for 264 yards with 2 touchdowns, while Ernie Caddel caught 9 passes for 127 yards with a touchdown.

10. Beattie Feathers. In 1934, as a rookie for the Chicago Bears, Feathers gained 1,004 yards with an NFL-best 8 touchdowns on 119 carries. His 8.4 yards per carry remain a league record (minimum 100 carries). He also had 6 receptions for 174 yards with a touchdown. He never came close to those numbers again. In 1935 with the Bears, he had 56 rushes for 281 yards with 3 touchdowns, and in 1936 for the Bears he ran the ball 97 times for 350 yards with 2 touchdowns. In one more season with Chicago, two with the Brooklyn Dodgers, and one with the Green Bay Packers, Feathers's rushing numbers got worse each season. He was the ultimate "one-year wonder."

11. They both had winning records, 6-4-2 for each, but finished in last place in the Western Division, a game behind both the first-place Detroit Lions and second-place Green Bay Packers. It remains the only time in history that any team finished in last place with a winning record. The following are the Western Division standings that year:

Team	W	L	T	Pct.
Detroit Lions	7	3	2	.700
Green Bay Packers	8	4	0	.667
Chicago Bears	6	4	2	.600
Chicago Cardinals	6	4	2	.600

The Bears outscored their opponents 192–106, while the Cardinals outscored their opponents 99–97. The two teams did not play one another until the last two games of the season.

The Bears began the season with a 7–0 loss to the Green Bay Packers. They won their next three games, but then fell to the Packers again 17–14. They beat the New York Giants 20–3 and the Boston Redskins 30–14. They lost to the Giants 3–0, tied the Detroit Lions 20–20, then lost to the same Lions 14–2. The Cardinals began their season by defeating the Packers 7–6, tying the Lions 10–10, and beating the Packers again 3–0. They split their next six games before beating the Packers again 9–7.

The Bears and Cardinals met for the first time on December 1 at Wrigley Field. Bronko Nagurski's 1-yard touchdown run in the second quarter gave the Bears a 7–0 lead. The Cardinals tied the score 7–7 in the fourth quarter on a 1-yard touchdown run by Al Nichelini. That is how the game ended. A week later, on December 8 in the season finale, the Bears and Cardinals squared off again at Wrigley Field. The Bears took a 6–0 first-quarter lead when Keith Molesworth ran for a 2-yard touchdown. Molesworth rushed for a 19-yard touchdown in the fourth quarter as the Bears won 13–0.

12. Detroit Lions. The Lions began the season with a 35–0 pounding of the Philadelphia Eagles. Two losses and a tie

in their next four games left them with a 2-2-1 record on October 20. Then they beat the Boston Redskins 14–0 and the Chicago Cardinals 7–6 before falling to the Packers 31–7 at Green Bay. In that game, the Packers took a 3–0 first-quarter lead on a 30-yard field goal by Clarke Hinkle. In the second quarter, George Sauer rushed for a touchdown as the Packers increased their lead to 10–0. Later in the quarter, Pug Vaughan threw a 28-yard touchdown pass to Ed Klewicki to pull the Lions within 10–7 at halftime. In the third quarter, Arnie Herber completed a 26-yard touchdown pass to Johnny Blood to up the Green Bay lead to 17–7. In the fourth quarter, Herber and Blood hooked up again on a 70-yard touchdown pass play to make the score 24–7. Herber hit Don Hutson on a 44-yard touchdown pass for the game's final points.

Seven days later at the University of Detroit Stadium, the Lions exacted some revenge by defeating the same Packers 20–10. Ernie Smith gave Green Bay a 3–0 first-quarter lead on a 22-yard field goal. In the second quarter, Dutch Clark threw a 20-yard touchdown pass to Harry Ebding as Detroit forged ahead 6–3 at halftime. Green Bay went back on top in the third quarter on a 9-yard touchdown pass from Sauer to Milt Gantenbein. In the fourth quarter, two short touchdown runs by Bill Shepherd were the game's final points. Detroit concluded the season with a 20–20 tie with the Chicago Bears, a 14–2 win over the same Bears, and a 28–0 triumph over the Brooklyn Dodgers on December 1.

Overall for the Lions, Glenn Presnell was 15-of-45 for 193 yards with 6 interceptions. Clark was 11-of-26 for 133 yards with 2 touchdowns and 4 interceptions. He ran the ball 120 times for 427 yards with 4 touchdowns and had 9 receptions for 124 yards with 2 touchdowns. Ernie Caddel had 87 rushes for 450 yards with 6 touchdowns and had 10 receptions for 171 yards.

The Lions, champions of the Western Division by percentage points over the Packers, met the Eastern Division champion New York Giants in the NFL title game on December 15 at home. The Lions took a 13–0 lead after one quarter on a 2-yard touchdown run by Ace Gutowsky and a 40-yard touchdown run by Clark. The Giants cut their deficit to 13–7 at halftime on a 42-yard touchdown pass from Ed Danowski to Ken Strong. In the fourth quarter, Caddel and Buddy Parker each had 4-yard touchdown runs as the Lions won 26–7.

13. c. 1936. The following are the final standings that year and the mishmash that was the final standings in the APFA's first season in 1920:

1936

Eastern Division

Team	W	L	T	Pct.
Boston Redskins	7	5	0	.583
Pittsburgh Pirates	6	6	0	.500
New York Giants	5	6	1	.455
Brooklyn Dodgers	3	8	1	.273
Philadelphia Eagles	1	11	0	.083

Western Division

Team	W	L	T	Pct.
Green Bay Packers	10	1	1	.909
Chicago Bears	9	3	0	.750
Detroit Lions	8	4	0	.667
Chicago Cardinals	3	8	1	.273

1920

Team	W	L	T	Pct.
Akron Pros	8	0	3	1.000
Decatur Staleys	10	1	2	.909
Buffalo All-Americans	9	1	1	.900
Rock Island Independents	6	2	2	.750

Chicago Cardinals	6	2	2	.750
Dayton Triangles	5	2	2	.714
Rochester Jeffersons	6	3	2	.667
Canton Bulldogs	7	4	2	.636
Detroit Heralds	2	3	3	.400
Cleveland Tigers	2	4	2	.333
Chicago Tigers	2	5	1	.286
Hammond Pros	2	5	0	.286
Columbus Panhandles	2	6	2	.250
Muncie Flyers	0	1	0	.000

14. d. Chicago Bears. After opening the season with a 10–7 win over the Chicago Cardinals, the Packers lost 30–3 to the Bears at home on September 20. It was all Bears from the start. Gene Ronzani broke a 3–3 second-quarter tie with a 12-yard touchdown run off a lateral for a 10–3 Chicago halftime lead. In the third quarter, Bill Hewitt caught a 12-yard touchdown pass from Ray Nolting to increase the Bears' lead to 16–3. In the fourth quarter, Carl Brumbaugh caught a 5-yard touchdown pass from Keith Molesworth to make the score 23–3. The game's final points came on a 9-yard touchdown run by Bill Karr.

Green Bay won its next nine games, including a 42–10 beating of the Pittsburgh Pirates on October 25 at the Wisconsin State Fair Park. Down 3–0 in the first quarter, Green Bay took a 7–3 lead on a 12-yard touchdown pass from Bob Monnett to Joe Laws. Three touchdowns in the second quarter, including a 58-yard pick-six by Johnny Blood, upped the Packers' lead to 28–3 at halftime. In the third quarter, Blood threw a 7-yard touchdown pass to Paul Miller, and Arnie Herber completed an 11-yard touchdown pass to Don Hutson. Pittsburgh scored a fourth-quarter touchdown for the game's final points. The Packers ended the season with a scoreless tie against the Cardinals and were Western Division champions.

Overall for the Packers, Herber was 77-of-173 for 1,239 yards with 11 touchdowns and 13 interceptions. Clarke Hinkle rushed the ball a hundred times for 476 yards with 5 touchdowns. Hutson had 34 receptions for 536 yards with 8 touchdowns.

In the NFL title game on December 13 at the Polo Grounds in New York, the Packers faced the Eastern Division champion Boston Redskins who finished with just a 7-5 record. In the first quarter, Green Bay took a 7–0 lead on a 48-yard touchdown pass from Herber to Hutson. The Redskins cut the lead to 7–6 in the second quarter on a short touchdown run by Pug Rentner. The Packers increased their lead to 14–6 in the third quarter on an 8-yard touchdown pass from Herber to Milt Gantenbein. In the fourth quarter, Bob Monnett scored on a 2-yard run for the game's final points in a 21–6 Green Bay victory.

15. Washington. The Redskins opened the season by beating the New York Giants 13–3 at home in Griffith Stadium. They lost two of their next three games and took a 2-2 record into an October 17 matchup at home against the Pittsburgh Pirates. In that game, Washington took a 7–0 first-quarter lead when Cliff Battles returned an interception 65 yards for a touchdown. In the second quarter, Pittsburgh tied the score on a 43-yard touchdown pass from Max Fiske to Johnny Blood. The Pirates went up 13–7 later in the quarter on a 55-yard touchdown pass from Blood to Tuffy Thompson. The Redskins tied the score in the third quarter when Sammy Baugh completed a 7-yard touchdown pass to Charley Malone. They took a 20–13 lead later in the third on a short touchdown pass from Riley Smith to Ed Justice. They put the game on ice in the fourth quarter when Battles ran for 60- and 62-yard touchdown runs. They went on to win 34–20.

Washington won four of its next five games and carried a 7-3 record into the season finale against the 6-2-2 Giants on December 5 at the Polo Grounds. The winner would be crowned Eastern Division champion and would face the Chicago Bears in the NFL title game. It was all Redskins from the start. Battles had two short touchdown runs in the first quarter to give them a 14–0 lead. They were up 28–14 after three quarters. Wayne Milner's recovery of a blocked punt in the end zone upped the visitor's lead to 35–14. They went on to win 49–14. They finished with an 8-3 record.

Overall in 1937, Baugh was 81-of-171 for 1,127 yards with 8 touchdowns and 14 interceptions. Battles had 216 rushes for 874 yards with 5 touchdowns. Malone had 28 receptions for 419 yards with 4 touchdowns.

In the championship game on December 12 at Wrigley Field, Battles scored on a 7-yard run to give Washington a 7–0 first-quarter lead. By the end of the first quarter, though, the Bears had a 14–7 lead. Three touchdown passes by Baugh in the third quarter—55 yards and 78 yards to Wayne Millner and 35 yards to Justice—led the Redskins to a 28–21 victory.

16. Rams. The Rams finished 1-10, in the far reaches of the Western Division basement that season. They were outscored 207–75 by their opponents. They began the season with a 28–0 defeat to the Detroit Lions on September 10 at League Park in Cleveland. Of Detroit's 4 touchdowns, 2 came on defense—a fumble recovery in the end zone by Harry Ebding and a 45-yard interception return by Tom Hupke. The Rams' only win of the season came by 21–3 in their second game on September 21 against the almost equally inept Eagles. In that game, played before just 3,107 fans at Philadelphia Municipal Stadium, the Rams took a 7–0 second-quarter lead on a 38-yard touchdown pass from Bob Snyder to Johnny Drake. The Eagles pulled to within 7–3 at halftime on a 12-yard field goal by Dave Smukler. In the fourth quarter, Snyder and Drake hooked up again on a 25-yard touchdown pass for a 14–3 Cleveland lead. The

Sammy Baugh, 1937
Harris & Ewing/Library of Congress

Rams put the game on ice when Joe Keeble caught a 42-yard touchdown strike from Harry Mattos.

In the next three games, Cleveland lost to the Brooklyn Dodgers (9–7), the Chicago Cardinals (6–0), and the Chicago Bears (20–2) to drop to 1-4. Next came a home matchup with Green Bay on October 17. The Packers took a 7–0 second-quarter lead when Don Hutson caught a 5-yard touchdown pass from Arnie Herber. The Rams cut it to 7–3 later in the second on a 30-yard field goal by Snyder. The Packers upped their lead to 14–3 by halftime on a 35-yard touchdown pass from Bob Monnett to Hutson. In the third quarter, Hutson caught another 35-yard scoring strike, this one from Herber to make the score 21–3. In the fourth quarter, Drake scored on a short touchdown run to pull the Rams within 21–10, but touchdown runs by Clarke Hinkle and Joe Laws were the daggers to the Rams' heart in Green Bay's 35–10 rout. The Rams lost all five of their remaining games, scoring exactly seven points in each one, the closest of which was 13–7 to the Cardinals.

Overall for Cleveland in 1937, Snyder was 25-of-66 for 378 yards with 2 touchdowns and 6 interceptions. He ran the ball 82 times for 232 yards with a touchdown. Drake had 98 carries for 333 yards with 3 touchdowns and 10 receptions for 172 yards with 2 touchdowns.

17. The Pittsburgh Pirates and the Detroit Lions. A consensus All-American in 1937 for the University of Colorado, White played for the Pirates in 1938 and for the Lions in 1940 and 1941. In 1938, he rushed the ball 152 times for a league-leading 567 yards with 4 touchdowns and had 7 receptions for 88 yards. He also was 29-of-73 for 393 yards with 2 touchdowns and a league-high 18 interceptions. In 1940, he ran the ball 146 times for a league-best 514 yards and caught 4 passes for 55 yards. He also was 35-of-80 for 461 yards with 12 interceptions. In 1941, he had 89 rushes for 240 yards with 2 touchdowns and 5 receptions for 158 yards with a touchdown. He also was 22-of-62 for 338

yards with 2 touchdowns and 5 picks. He returned punts and kickoffs, too, that year. He returned 19 punts for 262 yards, including a 64-yarder, and returned 11 kickoffs for 285 yards.

White's NFL career was cut short when he entered the U.S. Navy in 1942. After World War II, he chose to finish law school at Harvard University, where he had first attended during the 1939–40 school year, rather than return to football. He used the money he earned playing football to pay his law school tuition.

18. d. New York Giants, Washington Redskins. The game was played at the Polo Grounds on December 4. The Giants entered with a 7-2-1 record, while the Redskins were 6-2-2. The Redskins didn't know what hit them. From the start, the Giants poured it on. They took a 7–0 first-quarter lead when Hank Soar ran for a 43-yard touchdown. Later in the quarter, Bull Karcis ran for a touchdown to make the score 14–0. In the third quarter, Ward Cuff kicked a 36-yard field goal and returned an interception 96 yards for a touchdown to increase the New York lead to 24–0. In the fourth quarter, Chuck Gelatka caught a touchdown pass from Tuffy Leemans and had a 7-yard pick-six as the Giants won 36–0.

New York's opponent in the December 11 NFL Championship game, also at the Polo Grounds, was the Western Division champion Green Bay Packers. The Giants took a 9–0 lead after one quarter on a 14-yard field goal by Cuff and a 6-yard touchdown run by Leemans. The Packers cut their deficit to 9–7 in the second quarter on a 40-yard touchdown pass from Arnie Herber to Carl Mulleneaux. Later in the quarter, the Giants upped their lead to 16–7 on a 21-yard touchdown pass from Ed Danowski to Charles Barnard. The Packers cut it to 16–14 at halftime when Clarke Hinkle scored on a 1-yard touchdown run. They took a 17–16 lead in the third quarter on a 15-yard field goal by Tiny Engebretsen. Later in the third, Soar caught a

23-yard touchdown pass from Danowski for the final points in a 23–17 Giants' triumph.

19. The Green Bay Packers. The Packers finished with a record of 9-2 and won the Western Division Championship by a game over the Chicago Bears. They began the season with wins over both of Chicago's teams—the Cardinals and then the Bears. Then they lost 27–24 at home to the Cleveland Rams before winning three straight games over the Cardinals, Detroit Lions, and Washington Redskins. Then came a 30–27 loss to the Bears on November 5 in their first road game of the season. In that game, the Packers took a 7–0 first-quarter lead when Joe Laws returned a punt 72 yards for a touchdown. Later in the quarter, the Bears tied the score on a 57-yard touchdown run by Bob Swisher. Green Bay took a 13–7 lead after one quarter on a 32-yard touchdown pass from Cecil Isbell to Milt Gantenbein. At halftime, the Packers were up 20–17. The Bears took a 23–20 lead in the third quarter when Bernie Masterson threw an 8-yard touchdown pass to Dick Plasman. In the fourth quarter, Green Bay forged back ahead 27–23 on a 20-yard touchdown pass from Arnie Herber to Don Hutson. Bill Osmanski's short touchdown run gave the Bears the lead again and was the game's final points. The Packers won their final four games.

Overall for Green Bay in 1939, Herber was 57-of-139 for 1,107 yards with 8 touchdowns and 9 interceptions. Isbell was 43-of-103 for 749 yards with 6 touchdowns and 5 interceptions. He also ran the ball 132 times for 407 yards with 2 touchdowns. Clarke Hinkle had 135 rushes for 381 yards with 5 touchdowns. Hutson caught 34 passes for 846 yards with 6 touchdowns.

In the championship game on December 10 at home against the Eastern Division champion New York Giants, the Packers rolled. They took a 7–0 first-quarter lead on a 7-yard touchdown pass from Herber to Gantenbein. They upped their lead to 10–0 in the third quarter when Tiny

Engebretsen kicked a 29-yard field goal. Later in the third, Laws caught a 31-yard touchdown pass from Isbell to make it 17–0. In the fourth quarter, Ernie Smith booted a 42-yard field goal, and Ed Jankowski had a 1-yard touchdown run for the game's final points in a 27–0 Green Bay rout.

20. Clarke Hinkle and Bronko Nagurski. Hinkle played for the Packers from 1932 through 1941. In his rookie year, he had 95 rushes for 331 yards with 3 touchdowns. In 1934, he ran the ball 144 times for 359 yards with a touchdown and had 11 receptions for 113 yards with a touchdown. Two years later, he had 100 carries for 476 yards with 5 touchdowns. In that season's NFL Championship game, a 21–6 win over the Boston Redskins, Hinkle had 16 rushes for 58 yards. In 1937, he ran the ball 129 times for 552 yards with a league-leading 5 touchdowns and caught 8 passes for 116 yards with 2 touchdowns. In the 1938 NFL title game, a 23–17 defeat to the New York Giants, he had 18 rushes for 64 yards, including a 1-yard touchdown run in the second quarter. He was also a kicker and connected on an NFL-high 9-of-14 field-goal attempts in 1940 and a league-best 6-of-14 field-goal tries in 1941.

Overall, Hinkle had 1,171 rushes for 3,860 yards with 35 touchdowns and had 49 receptions for 537 yards with 9 touchdowns. He was a Pro Bowler from 1938 through 1940 and was enshrined into the Pro Football Hall of Fame in 1964.

Nagurski played for the Chicago Bears from 1930 through 1937 and in 1943. In 1932, he rushed the ball 121 times for 533 yards with a league-leading 4 touchdowns and had 6 receptions for 67 yards. He also was 11-of-26 for 150 yards with 3 touchdowns. The next year, he had 128 rushes for 533 yards with a touchdown. He also was 14-of-27 for 233 yards. In that year's NFL Championship game, a 23–21 victory over the New York Giants, he gained 64 yards on 13 carries and completed both of his passes for 42 yards with a touchdown. In 1934, he ran the ball 123 times for 586 yards with 7 touchdowns. In the NFL title game that year, a 30–13 loss to the Giants, he had 24 rushes for 68 yards with a touchdown. In 1936, he had 122 rushes for 529 yards with 3 touchdowns.

Overall, Nagurski had 633 rushes for 2,778 yards with 25 touchdowns. He was inducted into the Pro Football Hall of Fame's inaugural class of 1963.

THE 1940s

NEW RULES, A FASTER GAME, AND GROWING POPULARITY

After years of struggle, the NFL in the 1940s began to carve a niche in the American sports fandom. The action, the power on defense, and the variety and cleverness of attack shown by football's best players provided fans with higher standards of performance. Rule changes to make the game more exciting were another reason that attendance figures across the league began to soar.

QUESTIONS

1. What were the major rule changes for the 1940 NFL season? *Answer on page 47.*

2. What two teams played in the 1940 NFL Championship game? *Answer on page 47.*

3. In the Brooklyn Dodgers/Tigers' fifteen-year history, from 1930 through 1944, the team's best record was in 1940. What was it? *Answer on page 48.*

   a. 8-3

   b. 8-4

   c. 7-3

   d. 6-4-1

4. I was named the NFL's first commissioner on March 1, 1941. Who am I? *Answer on page 50.*

5. The 1941 season was the first in which there was a tie for first place. What two teams tied for first in the Western Division? *Answer on page 51.*

   a. Chicago Bears, Chicago Cardinals

   b. Green Bay Packers, Chicago Bears

   c. Cleveland Rams, Green Bay Packers

   d. Detroit Lions, Chicago Bears

6. Everyone remembers the Detroit Lions finishing 0-16 in 2008. Sixty-six years earlier, in 1942, there was another Lions team that was winless. What was their record? *Answer on page 52.*

   a. 0-9

   b. 0-10

   c. 0-11

   d. 0-12

7. In 1942, I shattered NFL records with 74 receptions, 1,211 receiving yards, and 17 touchdown catches. My initials are D.H. Who am I? *Answer on page 53.*

8. In 1943, the _____ and the _____ tied for first place in the Eastern Division with 6-3-1 records. *Answer on page 53.*

9. Sid Luckman was the first NFL quarterback to pass for _____ touchdowns in one game when he did it against the New York Giants on November 14, 1943, at the Polo Grounds. *Answer on page 54.*

    a. 4

    b. 5

    c. 6

    d. 7

10. Twice, during World War II, the Pittsburgh Steelers experienced a shortage of players. During the 1943 season, they merged with the Philadelphia Eagles, forming the "Phil-Pitt Eagles," and were known as the "Steagles." That team finished with a 5-4-1 record and in third place in the Eastern Division. Some home games were played at Shibe Park in Philadelphia and some at Forbes Field in Pittsburgh. With what team did the Steelers merge for the 1944 season? *Answer on page 55.*

11. The New York Giants and Green Bay Packers played for the 1944 NFL Championship. Who won? *Answer on page 56.*

12. What team won the 1945 NFL Championship? *Answer on page 57.*

13. What two teams played for the 1946 NFL title? *Answer on page 59.*

14. The Philadelphia Eagles finished 8-4 and tied with the _____ for first place in the Eastern Division in 1947. *Answer on page 60.*

15. Who led the NFL in pass completions, pass attempts, passing yards, and touchdown passes in 1947? *Answer on page 61.*

    a. Tommy Thompson
    b. Sammy Baugh
    c. Sid Luckman
    d. Bob Waterfield

16. What Philadelphia Eagle led the NFL in rushes, rushing yards, and rushing touchdowns every season from 1947 through 1949? *Answer on page 62.*

17. What NFL team in 1948 became the first to place a design on its helmet? *Answer on page 62.*

18. The Chicago Cardinals and Chicago Bears were tied with 10-1 records heading into their finale against one another at Wrigley Field on December 12, 1948. The winner would be crowned Western Division champions. Who won? *Answer on page 63.*

19. The Philadelphia Eagles won their second consecutive NFL Championship in 1949. True or false? *Answer on page 63.*

20. The New York Bulldogs went winless in their expansion season of 1949. True or false? *Answer on page 64.*

ANSWERS

1. One was that the penalty for a forward pass not from scrimmage was 5 yards. Another was that penalties for fouls that occurred prior to a pass or kick from behind the line of scrimmage were enforced from the previous spot. However, penalties for fouls during a free ball or when the offensive team fouled behind the line of scrimmage were enforced from the spot of the foul. A third rule change was that fouls enforced in the field of play could not penalize the ball more than half the distance to the offender's goal line. The final one was that if the offensive team committed pass interference in their opponent's end zone the defense had the choice of 15 yards from the previous spot and a loss of down or a touchback.

2. The Washington Redskins and the Chicago Bears. The Redskins won the Eastern Division with a 9-2 record. They won their first seven games of the season before splitting their final four games. The Bears won the Western Division with an 8-3 record. The two teams met once during the regular season, a 7–3 Redskins victory on November 17 at Griffith Stadium in Washington before a crowd of 35,331.

   The championship game was played on December 8, again in Griffith Stadium before a crowd of 36,034. To say the game was all Chicago from the start is the understatement of the century. The Bears took a 7–0 first-quarter lead when Bill Osmanski ran for a 68-yard touchdown. Later in the quarter, Sid Luckman scored from a yard out. That was followed by a 42-yard touchdown run by Joe Maniaci for a 21–0 Bears lead after one quarter. By halftime, the score was 28–0. The visitors scored a field goal and 3 touchdowns in the third quarter, with each of the touchdowns coming on pick-sixes. The first was a 15-yarder by Hampton Pool, the second was a 34-yarder by George McAfee, and the third was a 24-yarder by Bulldog Turner. After three quarters, the Bears led 54–0. But they weren't done. They scored three more times in the fourth quarter, and by the end of the game, the score had ballooned to 73–0. The rout still ranks as the most one-sided game in NFL history.

The Bears outgained the Redskins 381–5 in rushing yards and 519–231 in total yards. The Bears committed only 1 turnover, while the Redskins had 9, 8 of them interceptions, 5 by Frank Filchock. Luckman was 3-of-4 for 88 yards with a touchdown. Bob Snyder completed all three of his passes for 31 yards. Osmanski had 10 rushes for 109 yards, Harry Clarke ran the ball 8 times for 73 yards with 2 touchdowns, including a 44-yarder, and Ray Nolting had 13 carries for 68 yards, including a 23-yard touchdown run. Joe Maniaci had 6 rushes for 60 yards, including a 42-yard touchdown run, and had 3 receptions for 39 yards, including a 24-yarder. Bob Swisher had a 35-yard reception.

Filchock was 7-of-23 for 87 yards. Sammy Baugh was 10-of-17 for 102 yards. Wayne Millner had 5 receptions for 84 yards, including a 52-yarder from Filchock. Charley Malone had 2 catches for 58 yards, including a 50-yarder from Baugh, and Bob Masterson caught 3 passes for 33 yards.

The game was the first NFL Championship contest carried on network radio, broadcast by Red Barber to 120 stations of the Mutual Broadcasting System, which paid $2,500 for the rights.

3. a. 8-3. The Dodgers finished a game behind the Washington Redskins in the Eastern Division. They opened the season with a 24–17 loss to the Redskins on September 15 at Griffith Stadium in Washington. In that game, the Redskins took a 7–0 first-quarter lead when Ed Justice caught a 41-yard touchdown pass from Sammy Baugh. Bo Russell's 25-yard touchdown run in the second quarter made it 17–0 at the half. The Dodgers cut their deficit to 17–10 after three quarters on a 9-yard touchdown pass from Ace Parker to Mike Gussie and a 30-yard field goal by Ralph Kercheval. In the fourth quarter, Dick Todd caught a short touchdown pass from Filchock to increase the Redskins' lead to 24–10.

Red Barber
World Telegram & Sun/*Library of Congress*

Brooklyn scored the game's final points on a 17-yard touchdown pass from Parker to Banks McFadden.

The Dodgers defeated the Pittsburgh Steelers twice and the Philadelphia Eagles before losing two of three games to fall to 4-3. Next was a rematch with the Redskins at Ebbets Field in Brooklyn on November 10 in front of 33,846 fans. In that game, Brooklyn took a 7–0 first-quarter lead when Rhoten Shetley caught a touchdown pass from Parker. The Dodgers scored a safety in the second quarter for a 9–0 half-time lead. They upped their lead to 16–0 in the third quarter on a 36-yard touchdown pass from George Cafego to Parker. The Redskins rallied in the fourth quarter on an 18-yard touchdown pass from Baugh to Bob Masterson and a 1-yard touchdown run by Bob Seymour, but it wasn't enough in Brooklyn's 16–14 triumph. The Dodgers won their last three games over the Cleveland Rams, Chicago Cardinals, and New York Giants.

4. Elmer Layden. Before going to the NFL, I starred at fullback from 1922 through 1924 as a member of the legendary "Four Horsemen" offensive backfield for the University of Notre Dame. I was inducted into the College Football Hall of Fame in 1951. I played professionally in the original American Football League in 1925 and 1926 with three teams— the Hartford Blues, the Brooklyn Horsemen, and the Rock Island Independents. I began my coaching career during the same two seasons as the head coach at Columbia College (now Loras College) in Dubuque, Iowa. I was then the head coach at Duquesne University from 1927 through 1933 and for my alma mater, Notre Dame, from 1934 through 1940, where I was also the athletic director. Overall, I compiled a 103-34-11 record.

I was the NFL commissioner through 1946. In my five years as commissioner, I saw the NFL through the World War II years, in which teams had to use many men of inferior abilities as replacements while most of the regulars were fighting in the war. I once conducted an investigation into a betting scam without advising the owners, which did not reveal any conspiracy. At the end of the war, after Japan announced it would surrender, I called for all of the league's teams to play "The Star-Spangled Banner" at their games, arguing, "The national anthem should be as much a part of every game as the kickoff. We must not drop it simply because the war is over. We should never forget what it stands for." Prior to this proclamation, "The Star-Spangled Banner" had not been officially required to be sung before the start of any NFL games.

5. b. Green Bay Packers, Chicago Bears. Both teams finished with a 10-1 record. The Bears defeated the Packers 25–17 in the two teams' first meeting in the regular season on September 28 at City Stadium in Green Bay. The Packers beat the Bears 16–14 in their second matchup in the regular season on November 2 at Wrigley Field in Chicago.

To break the tie and crown the Western Division champion, the Packers and Bears opposed one another on December 14 before 43,425 fans at Wrigley Field. Green Bay took a 7–0 first-quarter lead when Clarke Hinkle ran for a 1-yard touchdown. Later in the quarter, Chicago pulled within 7–6 on an 81-yard punt return for a touchdown by Hugh Gallarneau. The second quarter belonged to the Bears. First, Bob Snyder kicked a 24-yard field goal to give the home team a 9–7 lead. Then, Norm Standlee scored on 2 short touchdown runs to make it 23–7. Finally, Bob Swisher scored from 9 yards out for a 30–7 Bears' lead entering the fourth quarter. The final score was 33–14.

Chicago's George McAfee rushed the ball 14 times for 119 yards. Standlee had 15 carries for 79 yards.

Seven days later, on December 21 at Wrigley Field, the Bears took on the Eastern Division champion New York Giants in the NFL title game. With the score 9–9 in the third quarter, the Bears took control. Standlee had 2- and 7-yard touchdown runs to put Chicago on top 23–9 after three quarters. In the fourth quarter, the Bears put the game away when McAfee scored on a 5-yard touchdown run to make it 30–9. Ken Kavanaugh's 42-yard fumble return for a touchdown put the finishing touches on a 37–9 Chicago victory.

The Bears' Sid Luckman was 9-of-12 for 160 yards. Standlee had 17 rushes for 89 yards and 2 receptions for 34 yards. McAfee ran the ball 14 times for 81 yards and caught 2 passes for 42 yards.

6. c. 0-11. The Lions finished in the far reaches of the Western Division basement. They were outscored 263–38 by their opponents. They never scored more than seven points in a game. They began the season with losses to the Chicago Cardinals, Cleveland Rams, and Brooklyn Dodgers. In Week 4, on October 11 at Green Bay, the Lions took on the Packers. The Lions actually had an early 7–3 lead on a 9-yard touchdown run by Elmer Hackney. A 6-yard touchdown pass from Cecil Isbell to Andy Uram gave the Packers a 10–7 lead after one quarter. In the second quarter, Isbell connected with Don Hutson on touchdown passes of 69 yards and 20 yards to give Green Bay a 24–7 halftime lead. Chuck Sample had a 2-yard touchdown run in the third quarter, and Keith Ranspot caught a 25-yard touchdown pass from Tony Canadeo in the fourth quarter as Green Bay went on to win 38–7.

Five losses later came a matchup with the Chicago Bears on November 22 at Briggs Stadium in Detroit. It was all Bears from the start. Harry Clarke gave them a 7–0 first-quarter lead on a 26-yard touchdown run. He then caught a 43-yard touchdown pass from Sid Luckman for a 14–0 Chicago lead after one quarter. Touchdown passes from Charlie O'Rourke to Ray McLean (68 yards) and Hampton Pool (5 yards) upped the Bears' lead to 28–0 at halftime. Two more touchdown passes, one from Luckman to Hugh Gallarneau for 60 yards in the third quarter and the other from O'Rourke to John Siegal for 28 yards in the fourth quarter, were the game's final points in a 42–0 spanking. The Lions had 12 turnovers. They finished the season with a 15–3 loss at home to the Washington Redskins on November 29.

7. Don Hutson. I played for the Green Bay Packers from 1935 through 1945. In 1936, I had 34 receptions for 536 yards with 8 touchdowns in leading the Packers to the NFL Championship. In a 21–6 title-game win over the Boston Redskins, I had 5 receptions for 76 yards, including a 48-yard touchdown catch from Arnie Herber. In 1938, I had 32 catches for 548 yards with 9 touchdowns in helping the Packers return to the championship game, but we lost to the New York Giants. The next year, I caught 34 passes for 846 yards with 6 touchdowns in leading us to the NFL title. In 1941, I had 58 receptions for 738 yards with 10 touchdowns in helping us to a tie with the Chicago Bears for the Western Division Championship. We lost a playoff 33–14. In 1944, I had 58 catches for 866 yards with 9 touchdowns in leading us back to the NFL Championship. In a 14–7 title-game win over the Giants, I had 2 receptions for 47 yards.

Overall, I had 488 receptions for 7,991 yards with 99 touchdowns. I was picked for the Pro Bowl from 1939 through 1942 and was inducted into the Pro Football Hall of Fame in its inaugural class of 1963.

8. New York Giants, Washington Redskins. The two teams tangled in the regular-season finale at Griffith Stadium in Washington. The Redskins came into the game with a 6-2-1 record, and the Giants were 5-3-1. New York won, going away 31–7, forcing a playoff seven days later on December 19 at the Polo Grounds. This time, the Redskins won with ease 28–0. Andy Farkas scored on short touchdown runs in the second quarter to give Washington a 14–0 halftime lead. He had another short touchdown run in the fourth quarter to make it 21–0. Sammy Baugh threw an 11-yard touchdown pass to Ted Lapka for the game's final points.

The win by Washington set up an NFL Championship game matchup with the Western Division champion Chicago Bears on the day after Christmas at Wrigley Field. Before

34,320 fans, the Redskins took a 7–0 lead in the second quarter on a 1-yard touchdown run by Farkas. Sid Luckman threw a 31-yard scoring strike to Harry Clarke to tie the game. Bronko Nagurski's 3-yard touchdown run gave the Bears a 14–7 halftime lead. Two long touchdown passes from Luckman to Dante Magnani upped the Chicago lead to 27–7 in the third quarter. Farkas caught a 17-yard touchdown pass from Baugh to pull Washington within 27–14 after three quarters, but Luckman hit Clarke and Joe Aguirre for touchdown passes to put the game away en route to a 41–21 Redskins triumph.

9. d. 7. The Bears routed the Giants that day 56–7. Luckman threw a 4-yard touchdown pass to Jim Benton and a 31-yard touchdown pass to Connie Mack Berry to give the Bears a 14–0 lead after one quarter. After the Giants cut their deficit to 14–7 in the second quarter, Luckman threw a 27-yard touchdown pass to Hampton Pool as Chicago upped its lead to 21–7. By halftime, it was 28–7. In the third quarter, Luckman completed a 62-yard touchdown pass to Harry Clarke and a 15-yard touchdown pass to Benton to make the score 42–7 after three quarters. In the fourth quarter, Luckman threw a 3-yard touchdown pass to George Wilson and a 40-yard touchdown pass to Pool for the final points of the game. Since that day, seven other quarterbacks have thrown for 7 touchdowns in one game:

* Adrian Burk, Philadelphia Eagles—49–21 win over Washington Redskins (October 17, 1954)
* George Blanda, Houston Oilers—49–13 win over New York Titans (November 19, 1961)
* Y. A. Tittle, New York Giants—49–34 win over Washington Redskins (October 28, 1962)
* Joe Kapp, Minnesota Vikings—52–14 win over Baltimore Colts (September 28, 1969)
* Peyton Manning, Denver Broncos—49–27 win over Baltimore Ravens (September 5, 2013)

* Nick Foles, Philadelphia Eagles—49–20 win over Oakland Raiders (November 3, 2013)
* Drew Brees, New Orleans Saints—52–49 win over New York Giants (November 1, 2015)

Luckman played for the Bears from 1939 through 1950. In 1940, he was 48-of-105 for 941 yards with 4 touchdowns and 9 interceptions in leading the Bears to the NFL Championship. In a 73–0 rout of the Washington Redskins in the title game, he was 3-of-4 for 88 yards with a touchdown. In 1941, he was 68-of-119 for 1,181 yards with 9 touchdowns and 6 interceptions as the Bears won the NFL title again. In a 37–9 win over the New York Giants in the title game, he was 9-of-12 for 160 yards. In 1942, he led the Bears back to the league title game, but they lost to Washington. The next year, he was 110-of-202 for 2,194 yards with 28 touchdowns and 12 interceptions in leading Chicago to the NFL Championship. In a 41–21 victory over the Redskins in the title game, he was 15-of-26 for 286 yards with 5 touchdowns, and he ran the ball 8 times for 64 yards. In 1946, he was 110-of-229 for 1,826 yards with 17 touchdowns and 16 picks in leading the Bears to the NFL Championship. In a 24–14 win over the Giants in the title contest, he was 9-of-22 for 144 yards with a touchdown and 2 interceptions.

Overall, Luckman completed 904 of 1,744 passes for 14,686 yards with 137 touchdowns and 132 interceptions. He was a Pro Bowler from 1940 through 1942 and was inducted into the Pro Football Hall of Fame in 1965.

10. The Chicago Cardinals. The team, known as "Card-Pitt" or, mockingly, the "Carpets," finished with an 0-10 record and in last place in the Western Division. It got outscored by its opponents 328–108. Card-Pitt played some of its home games at Comiskey Park in Chicago and some at Forbes Field. The team's season opener was, by far, its closest game of the season. It was a 30–28 loss to the Cleveland Rams on September 24 at Forbes Field. After that, it was downhill.

The team lost two straight games by the same 34–7 score to the Green Bay Packers and the Chicago Bears. Then came the team's only shutout, a 23–0 loss to the New York Giants, which dropped its record to 0-4.

On October 29, Card-Pitt lost 42–20 to the Redskins in Washington. The Redskins took a 7–0 first-quarter lead when Frank Filchock completed a 58-yard touchdown pass to Joe Aguirre. In the second quarter, Filchock and Aguirre hooked up again on a 47-yard touchdown pass to make the score 14–0 at halftime. After John Grigas scored on a 1-yard run to pull Card-Pitt within seven points, Washington struck again when Wilbur Moore broke free for a 75-yard touchdown run to up the Redskins' lead to 21–7 after three quarters. Card-Pitt pulled within 21–20 on an 8-yard touchdown run by Grigas and a 7-yard touchdown pass from Grigas to Don Currivan. The Redskins then exploded for 3 touchdowns—a short run by Bob Seymour, a 23-yard pass from Filchock to Seymour, and a 35-yard pass from Sammy Baugh to Doug Turley for the final points of the game.

Next came two losses to the Detroit Lions and defeats to Cleveland and Green Bay before a season-ending game against the Bears on December 3 at Forbes Field. In that game, the Bears took a 7–0 lead in the first quarter on a 9-yard touchdown pass from Gene Ronzani to Connie Mack Berry. Jim Fordham's 1-yard touchdown run in the second quarter made it 14–0. Card-Pitt's lone tally came on a short touchdown run by Bob Thurbon to make the score 14–7. By the end of the third quarter, it was 21–7. In the fourth quarter, the Bears really poured it on. Touchdown runs by Bob Margarita, Fordham, and Bulldog Turner plus a 5-yard touchdown pass from Ronzani to Doug McEnulty gave them a 49–7 victory.

11. The Packers won 14–7 on December 17 at the Polo Grounds. The Giants won the Eastern Division Championship with an 8-1-1 record. They won their first three games

against the Boston Yanks, Brooklyn Tigers, and Card-Pitt before losing 24–17 at home to the Philadelphia Eagles. They beat the Yanks again before tying the Eagles 21–21 at Philadelphia. They won their last four games over Green Bay, Brooklyn, and the Washington Redskins twice. The Packers won the Western Division title with an 8-2 record. They began the season by winning their first six games, including two over the Detroit Lions. They split their last four games.

In the NFL Championship game, the Packers took a 7–0 second-quarter lead when Ted Fritsch scored on a 1-yard touchdown run. Fritsch increased the Packers' lead to 14–0 at halftime when he caught a 28-yard touchdown pass from Irv Comp. The Giants cut their deficit to seven points in the fourth quarter on a 1-yard touchdown run by Ward Cuff.

The Packers' Joe Laws had 13 rushes for 74 yards, while Fritsch ran the ball 17 times for 58 yards. Don Hutson had 2 receptions for 47 yards. For the Giants, Arnie Herber was 8-of-22 for 117 yards with 4 interceptions. Cuff had 12 rushes for 50 yards, and Frank Liebel had 3 receptions for 71 yards.

12. The Cleveland Rams. The Rams spent their very first season of existence, 1936, as a member of a short-lived American Football League. With Sid Gillman as a receiver, they finished 5-2-2 and in second place behind the Boston Shamrocks. They might have hosted the AFL Championship game at League Park, but the Boston team cancelled because its unpaid players refused to participate. The next year, the Rams moved to the better-established NFL.

In 1937, Cleveland finished 1-10 and in last place in the Western Division, its only win coming against the almost-as-pitiful Philadelphia Eagles. During the next five seasons, the Rams improved but not nearly enough to compete for the Western title. They failed to post even a winning record during that time span. The team suspended play in 1943 due to several players, and even majority owner Dan Reeves, getting drafted into the military. The Rams were back in business in 1944, and with players like Jim Benton, Steve Pritko, Jim Gillette, Tom Colella, Riley Matheson, and Mike Scarry leading the way, finished 4-6, including upsets of the Chicago Bears and Detroit Lions.

By 1945, the Rams were ready to contend for an NFL Championship. They began the season with shutout victories over the Chicago Cardinals and the Bears. They went on to win their first four games before getting beaten by the Eagles 28–14 on October 28 at Shibe Park in Philadelphia. Then came wins over the New York Giants, the Green Bay Packers, and the Cardinals to set up a huge matchup with the Lions at Briggs Stadium in Detroit, a venue where the Rams won the year before. Cleveland entered the game with a 7-1 record, and the Lions came in 6-2. Fred Gehrke gave the Rams a 7–0 first-quarter lead on a 23-yard touchdown run. With the score 7–7 in the second period, quarterback Bob Waterfield threw a 70-yard touchdown pass to Benton to give the Rams back the lead 14–7. Waterfield's short touchdown run upped Cleveland's lead to 21–7 at halftime. His 17-yard touchdown pass to Pritko made it 28–7 after three quarters. A late rally by Detroit was not enough as the Rams prevailed 28–21 and clinched the Western Division title. They finished the season 9-1.

Cleveland's opponent in the NFL Championship game was the Eastern Division champion Washington Redskins. The game was played on December 16 at Cleveland Municipal Stadium. After the Rams scored a safety to take a 2–0 first-quarter lead, the Redskins forged ahead 7–2 in the second quarter. Later in the second, Benton caught a 37-yard touchdown pass from Waterfield for a 9–7 Cleveland halftime lead. In the third quarter, Gillette caught a 44-yard touchdown pass from Waterfield to make the score 15–7. Later in the quarter, the Redskins scored a touchdown, but those were the final points of the game as the Rams won 15–14 and were NFL champions.

Incredibly, even though they had just won the NFL title, poor attendance, financial losses, and the specter of the new Cleveland Browns of the All-America Football Conference starting play in 1946 all contributed to the Rams relocating west to Los Angeles.

13. The New York Giants and the Chicago Bears. The Giants won the Eastern Division with a 7-3-1 record. They began the season with three road games, beating the Boston Yanks and the Pittsburgh Steelers and then losing to the Washington Redskins. They beat the Chicago Cardinals and the Bears at home before falling to the Eagles in Philadelphia 24–14. The rest of the Giants' games were at home, beginning with a 45–17 rout of the Eagles the next week on November 10 to improve to 5-2. After that, they tied the Yanks 28–28 and then beat Pittsburgh, the Los Angeles Rams, and the Redskins to finish out the season.

The Bears won the Western Division crown with an 8-2-1 record. They started the season by winning road games at the Green Bay Packers and Cardinals before tying the Rams at home on October 13. They split their next two games and then reeled off four wins in a row, the last of which was a 42–6 pounding of the Detroit Lions, to improve to 7-1-1. They split their last two games of the season, losing to the Cardinals and beating the Lions.

The championship game was played on December 15 before 58,346 fans at the Polo Grounds. The Bears, trying to exact some revenge for their regular-season loss to the Giants in the same venue, drew first blood when Sid Luckman threw a 21-yard touchdown pass to Ken Kavanaugh in the opening quarter. Later in the quarter, Dante Magnani returned an interception 19 yards for a touchdown to up the visitor's lead to 14–0. The Giants cut their deficit to 14–7 after one quarter on a 38-yard touchdown pass from Frank Filchock to Frank Liebel. The Giants tied the game in the third quarter on a short touchdown pass from Filchock to Steve Filipowicz. In the fourth quarter, Luckman ran for a

19-yard touchdown, and Frank Maznicki booted a 26-yard field goal as the Bears went on to win 24–14.

Luckman was 9-of-22 for 144 yards with 2 interceptions. George McAfee had 4 receptions for 57 yards, while Kavanaugh had 2 catches for 53 yards. Filchock was 9-of-26 for 128 yards with 6 interceptions. George Franck rushed the ball 6 times for 55 yards. Filipowicz had 2 receptions for 41 yards, and Jim Poole caught 4 passes for 40 yards.

14. Pittsburgh Steelers. Despite finishing 8–4, the Steelers actually gave up more points than they scored, 259–240. The Steelers and Eagles battled in a playoff game on December 21 at Forbes Field in Pittsburgh to determine who would face the Western Division champion Chicago Cardinals in the NFL title game. It was all Philadelphia from the start. The Eagles took a 7–0 first-quarter lead when Tommy Thompson threw a 15-yard touchdown pass to Steve Van Buren. In the second quarter, Thompson completed a 28-yard touchdown pass to Jack Ferrante for a 14–0 Eagles halftime lead. Bosh Pritchard put the icing on the cake in the third quarter when he returned a punt 79 yards for a touchdown en route to a 21–0 Philadelphia victory.

Thompson was 11-of-17 for 131 yards. Van Buren had 18 rushes for 45 yards, while Ernie Steele ran the ball 6 times for 34 yards. Ferrante had 5 receptions for 73 yards. For Pittsburgh, Johnny Clement ran the ball 14 times for 59 yards. Elbie Nickel had 2 catches for 32 yards.

In the title game on December 28 at Comiskey Park in Chicago, the Cardinals took a 7–0 lead in the first quarter when Charley Trippi had a 44-yard touchdown run. In the second quarter, Elmer Angsman ran for a 70-yard touchdown to increase the Chicago lead to 14–0. Thompson threw a 53-yard touchdown pass to Pat McHugh to cut the Eagles' deficit to 14–7 at the half. In the third quarter, Trippi raced for a 75-yard touchdown to make the score 21–7. The Eagles cut it to 21–14 after three quarters on a 1-yard touchdown run by Van Buren. Angsman repeated his second-quarter feat by scoring on a 70-yard touchdown run to up the Cardinals' lead to 28–14. They went on to win 28–21.

Angsman ran the ball 10 times for 159 yards, while Trippi had 11 rushes for 84 yards. Billy Dewell had a single reception for 38 yards. Thompson was 27-of-44 for 297 yards with 3 interceptions. Ferrante had 8 catches for 73 yards, and McHugh had 2 receptions for 55 yards.

15. b. Sammy Baugh. "Slingin' Sammy" of the Washington Redskins was 210-of-354 for 2,938 yards with 25 touchdowns. All were career highs. He also had 15 interceptions. Before he turned pro, Baugh played for Texas Christian University from 1934 through 1936. He led TCU to two bowl-game wins, a 3–2 victory over LSU in the 1936 Sugar Bowl and a 16–6 triumph over Marquette in the first annual Cotton Bowl Classic in 1937, a game in which he was named Most Valuable Player. Baugh was an All-American his last two seasons.

In his rookie season with Washington in 1937, Baugh was 81-of-171 for 1,127 yards with 8 touchdowns and 14 interceptions in leading the Redskins to an 8-3 record and the Eastern Division Championship. They beat the Chicago Bears 28–21 in the NFL title game in which Baugh was 18-of-33 for 335 yards with 3 touchdowns and an interception. In 1940, he was 111-of-177 for 1,367 yards with 12 touchdowns and 10 interceptions. Washington won the Eastern Division Championship with a 9-2 record. They lost to the Bears 73–0 in the league title game. In that game, he was 10-of-17 for 102 yards with two picks. He led the Redskins to NFL Championship games in 1942, 1943, and 1945, with the 1942 team defeating the Bears 14–6. In 1945, he had a career-high passing percentage of 70.3 on 128 completions in 182 attempts. In 1948, he was 185-of-315 for 2,599 yards with 22 touchdowns and 23 interceptions.

Overall in his career, which lasted through 1952, Baugh completed 1,693 of 2,995 passes for 21,886 yards with 187 touchdowns and 203 interceptions. He was a Pro Bowler from 1938 through 1942 and in 1951. He was inducted into the Pro Football Hall of Fame in its charter class of 1963.

16. Steve Van Buren. In 1947, Van Buren had 217 rushes for 1,008 yards with 13 touchdowns and had 9 receptions for 79 yards in leading the Eagles to the NFL Championship game against the Chicago Cardinals. The Eagles lost 28–21. In 1948, Van Buren ran the ball 201 times for 945 yards with 10 touchdowns and had 10 catches for 96 yards in helping the Eagles to the NFL Championship. In a 7–0 title-game victory over the Cardinals, he had 26 carries for 98 yards, including a 5-yard touchdown run in the fourth quarter for the game's only points. The next season, he had 263 rushes for 1,146 yards with 11 touchdowns and had 4 receptions for 88 yards with a touchdown in helping Philadelphia to a second straight league title. In a 14–0 championship-game triumph over the Los Angeles Rams, he ran the ball 31 times for 196 yards, including a 49-yarder.

Prior to, and after, that sensational three-year run, Van Buren, who played for the Eagles from 1944 through 1951, also enjoyed success. In 1945, he had 143 rushes for 832 yards with 15 touchdowns and had 10 catches for 123 yards with 2 touchdowns. In 1950, he had 188 carries for 629 yards with 4 touchdowns, including a 108-yard game in a 33–0 win over the Washington Redskins on November 12.

Overall, Van Buren had 1,320 rushes for 5,860 yards with 69 touchdowns and 45 receptions for 523 yards with 3 touchdowns. He was enshrined into the Pro Football Hall of Fame in 1965.

17. The Los Angeles Rams. A Rams player painted rams horns on his helmet, a design that the team still uses today. Also, the number of jersey modifications continued to grow, with many teams starting to switch colors and trying to find the right color combination.

18. The Cardinals, 24–21. The Bears took a 7–0 first-quarter lead when Ken Kavanaugh caught a 15-yard touchdown pass from Johnny Lujack. After a 34-yard field goal by Pat Harder made the score 7–3 after one quarter, in the second period Lujack threw a 35-yard scoring strike to George Gulyanics for a 14–3 Bears halftime lead. In the third quarter, Harder ran for a short touchdown run to make it 14–10 entering the fourth quarter. Gulyanics upped the Bears' lead to 21–10 when he scored on a short touchdown run. Touchdown runs by Charley Trippi and Elmer Angsman were the game's final points.

Seven days later, on December 19 at Shibe Park in Philadelphia, the Cardinals and the Eastern Division champion Eagles tangled in the NFL Championship game. The contest was a scoreless tie until the fourth quarter when Steve Van Buren ran for a 5-yard touchdown en route to Philadelphia's 7–0 win.

The Eagles' Tommy Thompson ran the ball 11 times for 50 yards. Van Buren had 26 rushes for 98 yards, while Bosh Pritchard had 16 carries for 67 yards.

19. True. The Eagles finished with a record of 11-1 and won the Eastern Division by a mile over the Pittsburgh Steelers. They outscored their opponents 364–134. They beat the Western Division champion Los Angeles Rams in the NFL Championship game. The Eagles began the season with wins over the New York Bulldogs, Detroit Lions, and Chicago Cardinals. They experienced their only loss of the season on October 16, 38–21 to the Bears in Chicago, but a game that was not decided until the fourth quarter. After that, the Eagles won their last eight games, all by routs, the first six in which they hung up point totals of 49, 38, 38, 44, 42, and 34. They won their final two games against the New York Giants by scores of 24–3 and 17–3.

Overall for the Eagles in 1949, quarterback Tommy Thompson was 116-of-214 for 1,727 yards with 16 touchdowns and 11 interceptions. Steve Van Buren rushed the ball 263 times for 1,146 yards with 11 touchdowns. Bosh Pritchard had 84 rushes for 506 yards with 3 touchdowns. Jack Ferrante had 34 receptions for 508 yards with 5 touchdowns. Pete Pihos also had 34 catches, for 484 yards with 4 touchdowns. Neill Armstrong caught 24 passes for 271 yards with 5 touchdowns.

The NFL Championship game was played on December 18 at the Los Angeles Memorial Coliseum. Philadelphia dominated the Rams both in first downs, 17–7, and total yards, 342–119. The Eagles took a 7–0 second-quarter lead when Tommy Thompson completed a 31-yard touchdown pass to Pete Pihos. They went up 14–0 in the third quarter on a 2-yard return for a touchdown by Leo Skladany off a blocked punt. Those were the game's final points.

Steve Van Buren ran the ball 31 times for 196 yards, including a 49-yarder.

20. False. The Bulldogs finished with a record of 1-10-1 and, by far, in last place in the Eastern Division. They were outscored by their opponents 368–153. They began the season by putting up a good fight in a 7–0 loss to the defending NFL champion Philadelphia Eagles at home in the Polo Grounds. The next week, they were routed 38–14 by the New York Giants. The next three games they lost to the Green Bay Packers, Washington Redskins, and Pittsburgh Steelers. On October 30, they tied the Redskins 14–14, and they beat the Giants 31–24 the week after that.

Then came a 65–20 defeat at home to the Chicago Cardinals. In that game, the Cardinals took a 7–0 first-quarter lead when Jim Hardy threw a 19-yard touchdown pass to Charley Trippi. The Bulldogs tied the score after one quarter on a 13-yard touchdown pass from Bobby Layne to Joe Golding. In the second quarter, the Cardinals forged back ahead 14–7 on a short touchdown run by Pat Harder. Later in the quarter, Harder ran for a 42-yard touchdown to make the score 28–7. By halftime, it was 38–7. A pair of 12-yard touchdown passes from Paul Christman to Bob Ravensberg and Vic Schwall increased the lead to 52–7. Frank Muehl-heuser's 1-yard touchdown run made the score 52–13 after three quarters. Red Cochran caught a 41-yard touchdown pass from Christman and then ran for a 22-yard touchdown to make it 65–13 before John Rauch scored the game's final points on a 1-yard touchdown run. New York lost its remaining four games, the last of which was 27–0 at home to the Steelers.

Overall in 1949, Layne was 155-of-299 for 1,796 yards with 9 touchdowns and 18 interceptions. He ran the ball 54 times for 196 yards. Joe Osmanski had 66 rushes for 267 yards with 2 touchdowns and 17 receptions for 135 yards. Golding had 63 carries for 240 yards. Bill Chipley had 57 receptions for 631 yards with 2 touchdowns, while Ralph Heywood had 37 catches for 499 yards with 3 touchdowns.

THE 1950s

PRO FOOTBALL REACHES A NATIONAL AUDIENCE— ON TV

There were several changes with the NFL in the 1950s. After years of not allowing it, unlimited free substitution was restored in 1950, opening the way for the era of two platoons and specialization. The name National Football League was restored after about three months as the National-American Football League. Also in 1950, the American and National Conferences were created to replace the Eastern and Western Divisions. Three years later, though, they were changed to the Eastern and Western Conferences. Also in 1950, the All-America Football Conference merged three of its teams into the NFL.

The 1950 Los Angeles Rams became the first NFL team to have all of its games televised, but beginning in 1951, they decided to televise road games only. Other teams made deals to put selected games on television. In 1956, CBS became the first network to broadcast NFL regular-season games to selected television markets across the nation. Two years later, the Baltimore Colts–New York Giants Championship game had the first sudden-death overtime in a league title contest. The game, which was broadcast across the country by NBC, became known as "The Greatest Game Ever Played." It seemed to jumpstart enthusiasm for the NFL for fans across the country.

QUESTIONS

1. What three teams from the defunct All-America Football Conference joined the NFL in 1950? *Answer on page 71.*

2. Which West Coast team did the Cleveland Browns defeat in the 1950 NFL Championship game? *Answer on page 73.*

   a. Seattle Seahawks

   b. San Francisco 49ers

   c. Los Angeles Rams

   d. San Diego Chargers

3. What Los Angeles Rams player with the initials T.F. totaled 84 receptions in 1950, a record that stood for a decade? *Answer on page 73.*

4. I am a former Northwestern University player who signed with the Cleveland Browns as a free agent in 1946 and led them to seven championships in ten years, including four in the All-America Football Conference. Who am I? *Answer on page 74.*

5. What NFL record did the Cleveland Browns' Dub Jones tie on November 25, 1951, in a home game against the Chicago Bears? *Answer on page 74.*

6. Who led the NFL in completions, pass attempts, passing yards, and touchdown passes in 1951? *Answer on page 75.*

   a. Bobby Layne
   b. Otto Graham
   c. Norm Van Brocklin
   d. Charlie Conerly

7. In 1951, I led the NFL in receptions (66), receiving yards (1,495), and touchdown receptions (17). My nickname was "Crazy Legs." I also starred in several movies in the 1950s, including *Crazylegs*, *Unchained*, and *Zero Hour!* Who am I? *Answer on page 76.*

8. The Cleveland Browns and Los Angeles Rams opposed one another in the NFL Championship game for the second straight season in 1951. True or false? *Answer on page 77.*

9. The original Dallas Texans' lone year of existence was in 1952. They finished with a 1-11 record, by far the worst mark in the NFL. Against whom did their lone victory come? *Answer on page 77.*

   a. Philadelphia Eagles
   b. Chicago Bears
   c. Los Angeles Rams
   d. Pittsburgh Steelers

10. The _____ and _____ played for the 1952 NFL Championship. *Answer on page 78.*

11. The Philadelphia Eagles and Detroit Lions opposed one another in the 1953 NFL Championship game. True or false? *Answer on page 78.*

12. Who was the Detroit Lions' opponent in the 1954 NFL Championship game? *Answer on page 79.*

    a. Philadelphia Eagles
    b. New York Giants
    c. Chicago Bears
    d. Cleveland Browns

13. After four successful seasons, the Detroit Lions had a rough 1955 season in which they finished in last place in the Western Division. What was their record? *Answer on page 79.*

    a. 1-11
    b. 2-10
    c. 3-9
    d. 4-8

14. The Cleveland Browns defeated the Los Angeles Rams in the 1955 NFL Championship game. What was the score? *Answer on page 80.*

    a. 38–14
    b. 28–14
    c. 38–24
    d. 28–24

15. What two teams collided on the final day of the regular season with the 1956 Western Conference title on the line? *Answer on page 80.*

16. What Syracuse University product, who would spend nine amazing seasons with the Cleveland Browns as a fullback,

did the team choose in the first round of the 1957 NFL draft? *Answer on page 81.*

17. What two teams tied for first place in the Western Conference with 8-4 records, forcing a playoff game, in 1957? *Answer on page 83.*

18. The 1958 NFL Championship game was the first NFL postseason contest to go into sudden-death overtime. The Baltimore Colts defeated the New York Giants on December 28 at Yankee Stadium in New York. What was the final score? *Answer on page 84.*

   a. 20–14
   b. 16–13
   c. 23–17
   d. 30–27

19. What running back set an NFL record with 5 rushing touchdowns in one game on November 1, 1959? *Answer on page 85.*

   a. Alan Ameche
   b. Jim Brown
   c. Paul Hornung
   d. Ollie Matson

20. In 1959, the New York Giants and Baltimore Colts played one another in the NFL Championship game for the second year in a row. True or false? *Answer on page 85.*

ANSWERS

1. The Baltimore Colts, Cleveland Browns, and San Francisco 49ers. The Browns were the crown jewel of the three teams,

having won all four AAFC Championships with an overall record of 52-4-3 (including postseason) from 1946 through 1949. An innovator when it came to the game of football, Cleveland's Paul Brown was the first head coach to hire a full-time coaching staff, utilize classroom study to such a broad extent, use intelligence tests, grade his players from individual film clips, and develop a messenger-guard system so he could call plays from the sideline. He had much to do in inventing, or improving, plays such as the screen pass, draw play, and trap plays. He also invented the first single-bar facemask. The Browns also brought a sophisticated passing attack to the NFL.

Cleveland was tested right off the bat. The Browns' very first game in the NFL came on Saturday night, September 16, 1950, against the two-time defending champion Eagles. In front of 71,237 fans at Philadelphia Municipal Stadium, the Browns destroyed the heavily favored Eagles 35–10. After the Eagles took an early 3–0 lead, quarterback Otto Graham threw a 59-yard touchdown pass to Dub Jones to give the Browns a 7–3 lead after one quarter. Graham threw a 26-yard touchdown pass to Dante Lavelli for a 14–3 Cleveland half-time lead. The lead grew to 21–3 after three quarters when Mac Speedie caught a 13-yard scoring strike from Graham. The Eagles' only touchdown came in the fourth quarter on a 17-yard touchdown pass from Bill Mackrides to Pete Pihos. That was sandwiched by short touchdown runs by Graham and Rex Bumgardner.

The team statistics were even for the most part other than passing yards—the Browns outgained the Eagles in that department by more than 200 yards. Graham was 21-of-38 for 346 yards with 2 interceptions. Jones rushed the ball 6 times for 72 yards, including a 57-yarder, and had 5 receptions for 98 yards. Marion Motely had 11 carries for 48 yards. Speedie had 7 catches for 109 yards, and Lavelli caught 4 passes for 76 yards. Philadelphia's Frank Ziegler had 17 rushes for 57 yards, while Pihos had 4 receptions for 51 yards.

2. c. Los Angeles Rams. A week earlier, to reach the NFL title game, both teams won tiebreaker playoffs. The host Browns, who were 10-2 in the regular season, defeated the New York Giants 8–3 to win the American Conference, and the host Rams, who were 9-3 in the regular season, beat the Chicago Bears 24–14 to win the National Conference.

The Browns–Rams game, played on Christmas Eve in Cleveland Municipal Stadium, had many long plays. One was an 82-yard touchdown pass from Bob Waterfield to Glenn Davis to give Los Angeles a 7–0 first-quarter lead. The Browns pulled to within 14–13 at halftime on a 37-yard touchdown pass from Otto Graham to Dante Lavelli. Graham hit Lavelli again on a 39-yard scoring strike in the third quarter as the Browns took their first lead at 20–14. The Rams, though, had a 28–20 lead going into the fourth quarter. Graham, though, threw a 14-yard touchdown pass to Rex Bumgardner to pull the Browns within one point. Lou Groza kicked a 16-yard field goal with twenty-eight seconds left for the winning points in a 30–28 Browns' victory.

3. Tom Fears. In that 1950 season, his only Pro Bowl year, Fears had a league-leading 1,116 yards receiving with 7 touchdowns. He had 18 receptions in one game, a record that stood for half a century. He did it in a season-ending 51–14 rout of the Green Bay Packers, a game in which he also had 189 receiving yards with 2 touchdowns. In a 24–14 victory over the Chicago Bears in a National Conference playoff, he caught 3 touchdown passes from Bob Waterfield for 43 yards, 68 yards, and 27 yards. In total, he had 7 receptions for 198 yards. A week later, in a 30–28 loss to the Cleveland Browns in the NFL Championship game, he totaled 9 catches for 136 yards, including a 44-yarder from Waterfield.

In his rookie season with the Rams two years earlier, in 1948, Fears had a league-leading 51 receptions for 698 yards with 4 touchdowns. The next year, he had an NFL-high 77 catches for 1,013 yards with a league-best 9 touchdowns in helping the Rams advance to the NFL Championship game. In 1951, he missed five games but still managed 32 receptions for 528 yards with 3 touchdowns. In a 24–17 win over the Browns in the championship game, he had 4 receptions for 146 yards, including the game-winning 73-yard touchdown catch from Waterfield. The next year, he caught 48 passes for 600 yards with 6 touchdowns. In a 31–21 loss to the Detroit Lions in a National Conference playoff, he had 7 receptions for 76 yards, including a 14-yard touchdown pass from Norm Van Brocklin. His last hurrah came in 1955 when his 44 catches for 569 yards with 2 touchdowns helped Los Angeles advance to the NFL title game, which they lost to the Browns.

Fears retired after the 1956 season. Overall, he had 400 receptions for 5,397 yards with 38 touchdowns. He was inducted into the Pro Football Hall of Fame in 1970.

4. Otto Graham. I signed as a free agent and directed the Browns to four AAFC Championships from 1946 through 1949 and six NFL Championship games from 1950 through 1955, three of which we won. Even though I was not the starter in the Browns' very first game, I passed for 86 touchdowns and threw only 41 interceptions from 1946 through 1949 and won the AAFC passing title three times. I led Cleveland to NFL Championships in 1950 (over the Rams) and in 1954 and 1955 (over the Lions).

Overall, I completed 1,464 of 2,626 passes for 23,584 yards with 174 touchdowns and 135 interceptions. I was a Pro Bowler from 1950 through 1954. I was inducted into the Pro Football Hall of Fame in 1965.

5. Most touchdowns in one game. He scored 6 touchdowns in a 42–21 win over the Chicago Bears. He replaced an injured Marion Motley that day in Cleveland Municipal Stadium. He broke the team record of 4 touchdowns in a game, set by Dante Lavelli on October 14, 1949, and matched the feat of Ernie Nevers, who had 6 touchdowns on November 28, 1929.

Whereas Lavelli's and Nevers's touchdowns all came on receptions, Jones had 4 rushing touchdowns and 2 receiving touchdowns. Amazingly, all of his touchdowns were in the final three quarters (Chicago's Gale Sayers equaled Jones's and Nevers's accomplishment on December 12, 1965, when he had 4 rushing touchdowns, 1 receiving touchdown, and 1 touchdown on a punt return). In the third quarter, he had touchdown runs of 12 and 27 yards, respectively. In the fourth quarter, he had a 43-yard touchdown run and a 43-yard touchdown reception from Graham. Remarkably, the last five times he touched the ball, he scored. He ended up with 116 rushing yards on 9 carries and 80 receiving yards on 3 catches.

6. a. Bobby Layne. The Detroit Lions' star quarterback was 152-of-332 for 2,403 yards with 26 touchdowns. He also led the league with 23 interceptions. He spent his first season in 1948 as a backup with the Chicago Bears. The next season, he was the starter for the New York Bulldogs. In 1950 with Detroit, he was 152-of-336 for 2,323 yards with 16 touchdowns and 18 interceptions. In 1952, he was 139-of-287 for 1,999 yards with 19 touchdowns and 20 picks in leading the Lions to a 9-3 record and a tie with the Los Angeles Rams for first place in the National Conference. In a 31–21 victory over the Rams in a playoff, he was 9-of-21 for 144 yards with 4 interceptions. In a 17–7 win over the Cleveland Browns in the league title game, he was 7-of-9 for 68 yards and ran the ball 9 times for 47 yards, including a 2-yard touchdown run.

In 1953, Layne was 125-of-273 for 2,088 yards with 16 touchdowns and 21 interceptions as the Lions finished 10-2 and NFL champions. In a 17–16 win over Cleveland in the title game, he was 12-of-25 for 179 yards with a touchdown and two picks. The next season, he was 135-of-246 for 1,818 yards with 14 touchdowns and 12 interceptions in leading Detroit to a 9-2-1 record and an appearance in the NFL title game against the Browns. In 1957, he was 87-of-179 for 1,169 yards with 6 touchdowns and 12 interceptions as he split time at quarterback with Tobin Rote. The Lions finished 8-4 that year and tied the San Francisco 49ers for first place in the Western Conference. They beat the 49ers and Browns in the postseason to win the NFL Championship, but Layne did not see any action in those two games. He spent most of the 1958 season and the rest of his career, which lasted through 1962, with the Pittsburgh Steelers.

Overall, Layne completed 1,814 of 3,700 passes for 26,768 yards with 196 touchdowns and 243 interceptions. He was picked for the Pro Bowl from 1951 through 1953 and in 1956, 1958, and 1959. He was enshrined into the Pro Football Hall of Fame in 1967.

7. Elroy Hirsch. I played for the Los Angeles Rams that year. In that 1951 season, I had nine games in which I had at least 100 yards receiving. My biggest game that year was on November 11 when I had 6 catches for 195 yards with 2 touchdowns in a 45–21 win over the Chicago Cardinals. On opening day that year, I had 9 catches for 173 yards with 4 touchdowns in a 54–14 rout of the New York Yanks. On October 28, I caught 7 passes for 163 yards with a touchdown in a 44–17 loss to the San Francisco 49ers. I led the Rams to the NFL Championship. In a 24–17 win over the Cleveland Browns in the title game, I had 4 receptions for 66 yards.

I spent my first three seasons with the Chicago Rockets of the All-America Football Conference. I joined the Rams in 1949 and helped them advance to the NFL title game. In 1950, I had 42 receptions for 687 yards with 7 touchdowns as we finished 9-3 and tied the Chicago Bears for first place in the National Conference. In a 24–14 victory over the Bears in a playoff, I had 2 catches for 46 yards. In a 30–28 loss to Cleveland in the title game, I had 9 receptions for 136 yards, including a 44-yarder. In 1952, I played in only 7 games but still managed 25 catches for 590 yards with 4 touchdowns in helping the Rams to a 9-3 record and a tie for first place in the National Conference with the Detroit Lions. In a 31–21 defeat to the Lions in a playoff game, I had 5 receptions for 46 yards. I continued to have solid seasons the rest of my career, which lasted through 1957, including 25 catches for

460 yards with two touchdowns in helping Los Angeles advance to the 1955 NFL title game against the Browns.

Overall, I had 387 receptions for 7,029 yards with 60 touchdowns. I was a Pro Bowler from 1951 through 1953 and was inducted into the Pro Football Hall of Fame in 1968.

8. True. The Browns won the American Conference with an 11-1 record, and the Rams won the National Conference with an 8-4 mark. In the championship game, played on December 23 before 59,475 fans at the Los Angeles Memorial Coliseum, the Rams won 24–17. They took a 7–0 second-quarter lead when Dick Hoerner scored on a 1-yard touchdown run. Later in the quarter, Lou Groza's 53-yard field goal brought the Browns to within four points. They forged ahead 10–7 after one quarter when Otto Graham completed a 17-yard touchdown pass to Dub Jones. In the third quarter, the Rams went back ahead 14–10 on a short touchdown run by Dan Towler. Bob Waterfield upped the Los Angeles lead to 17–10 in the fourth quarter by kicking a 17-yard field goal. The Browns tied the score when Ken Carpenter ran for a 2-yard touchdown. The Rams' winning score came on a 73-yard touchdown pass from Norm Van Brocklin to Tom Fears.

Waterfield was 9-of-24 for 125 yards with 2 interceptions. Fears had 4 receptions for 146 yards, while Elroy Hirsch had 4 catches for 66 yards. Graham was 19-of-40 for 280 yards with 3 interceptions. He also ran the ball 5 times for 43 yards, including a 34-yarder. Mac Speedie had 7 receptions for 81 yards, Dante Lavelli had 4 catches for 65 yards, and Jones caught 4 passes for 62 yards.

9. b. Chicago Bears. The Texans beat the Bears 27–23 on Thanksgiving Day before three thousand fans at, believe it or not, the Rubber Bowl in Akron, Ohio. The Texans had lost their first nine games, with the closest margin being ten points in a 24–14 loss to the Green Bay Packers on October 18. In the win over the Bears, Chicago took the lead on a second-quarter safety. The Texans forged ahead 6–2 when

Zollie Toth had a 2-yard touchdown run. They took a 13–2 halftime lead when Dick Wilkins caught a 20-yard touchdown pass from George Taliaferro. The lead grew to 20–2 after three quarters on a short touchdown run by Frank Tripucka.

The Bears mounted a comeback, beginning with Billy Stone's 1-yard touchdown run to cut their deficit to 20–9. George Blanda then threw 2 touchdown passes—41 yards to Babe Dimancheff and 35 yards to Gene Schroeder—as Chicago forged ahead 23–20. The Texans took back the lead on another short touchdown run by Tripucka for the game's final points. They were blown out by the Philadelphia Eagles and Detroit Lions in their final two games.

10. Cleveland Browns, Detroit Lions. The Browns won the American Conference with an 8-4 record. The Lions tied the Los Angeles Rams for first place in the National Conference with a 9-3 record. The Lions beat the Rams in a playoff 31–21. The league title game was played on December 28 at Cleveland Municipal Stadium. Detroit took a 14–0 second-quarter lead on a 2-yard touchdown run by Bobby Layne and a 67-yard touchdown run by Doak Walker en route to a 17–7 victory.

Layne was 7-of-9 for 68 yards. He ran the ball 9 times for 47 yards. Walker ran the ball 10 times for 97 yards. For Cleveland, Otto Graham was 20-of-35 for 191 yards with an interception. Chick Jagade rushed the ball 15 times for 104 yards. Marion Motley had 6 carries for 74 yards, including a 42-yarder, and had 3 receptions for 21 yards. Pete Brewster had 2 receptions for 53 yards, including a 32-yarder from Graham.

11. False. The Cleveland Browns played Detroit in the league title game. The Browns won the Eastern Conference going away with an 11-1 record, while the Lions took the Western Conference crown with a 10-2 mark. The championship game was played on December 27 at Briggs Stadium in Detroit. Doak Walker gave the Lions a 7–0 first-quarter

lead when he scored from a yard out. The teams traded field goals in the second quarter, and the Lions led 10–3 at the half. Chick Jagade's 9-yard touchdown run in the third quarter tied the game 10–10. Two Lou Groza field goals in the fourth quarter put the Browns ahead 16–10, but Bobby Layne's 33-yard touchdown pass to Jim Doran gave the Lions a 17–16 victory.

Layne was 12-of-25 for 179 yards with 2 interceptions. He ran the ball 9 times for 44 yards. Doran caught 4 passes for 95 yards, while Cloyce Box had 4 catches for 54 yards. Jagade rushed the ball 15 times for 102 yards, including a 30-yarder, and had an 18-yard reception. Dub Jones had 3 carries for 28 yards, including a 19-yarder.

12. d. Cleveland Browns. The Browns won the Eastern Conference with a 9-3 record, while the Lions won the Western Conference with a 9-2-1 mark. The title game was played on December 26 at Cleveland Municipal Stadium. The Browns took a 14–3 lead after one quarter. Otto Graham had two short touchdown runs and a 31-yard touchdown pass to Ray Renfro as the Cleveland lead grew to 35–10 by halftime on the way to a 56–10 rout.

13. c. 3-9. They began the season by losing their first six games, the last of which was by a score of 38–21 to the 49ers on October 30 at Kezar Stadium in San Francisco. The 49ers took a 14–0 lead after one quarter on short touchdown runs by Joe Perry and Hugh McElhenny. The Lions pulled to within 14–7 in the second quarter on a 24-yard touchdown pass from Bobby Layne to Doak Walker. Gordie Soltau's 25-yard field goal later in the quarter upped the San Francisco lead to 17–7. The score ballooned to 24–7 on an 11-yard touchdown run by Dicky Moegle. Y. A. Tittle's 78-yard touchdown pass to Carroll Hardy made it 31–7 at the half. The 49ers put it in cruise control the rest of the way.

Beginning with a 24–14 win over the Baltimore Colts, the Lions won three of their next four games before falling to the Chicago Bears 21–20 and the New York Giants

24–19 to end the season. In the loss to the Giants, played on December 11 at Briggs Stadium in Detroit, the Lions took a 7–0 first-quarter lead when Harry Gilmer threw a 25-yard touchdown pass to Walker. Alex Webster's 6-yard touchdown run tied the score 7–7 after one quarter. In the second quarter, Frank Gifford ran for a 22-yard touchdown and caught a 37-yard touchdown pass from Don Heinrich for a 21–7 Giants' lead. It was 21–10 at halftime. Ben Agajanian kicked a 24-yard field goal in the third quarter to increase the New York lead to 24–10. The Lions rallied late, but it was not enough.

14. a. 38–14. The Browns won the Eastern Conference title with a 9-2-1 record, while the Rams won the Western Conference crown with an 8-3-1 mark. The championship game was played on December 26 at the Los Angeles Memorial Coliseum. The Browns took a 3–0 lead after the first quarter when Lou Groza kicked a 26-yard field goal. In the second quarter, Don Paul returned an interception 65 yards for a touchdown to up the Cleveland lead to 10–0. Later in the quarter, the Rams pulled to within 10–7 on a 67-yard touchdown pass from Norm Van Brocklin to Skeets Quinlan. The Browns increased their lead to 17–7 at halftime on a 50-yard touchdown pass from Otto Graham to Dante Lavelli. They put the game away in the third quarter when Graham ran for 2 touchdowns to make the score 31–7. Each team scored a meaningless touchdown in the fourth quarter.

Graham was 14-of-25 for 209 yards with 2 touchdowns and 3 interceptions. Ed Modzelewski had 13 rushes for 61 yards and 5 receptions for 34 yards. Lavelli had 3 receptions for 95 yards, while Ray Renfro had 2 catches for 49 yards, including a 35-yarder for a touchdown. Van Brocklin was 11-of-25 for 166 yards with 6 interceptions. Dan Towler had 14 rushes for 64 yards, while Quinlan had 5 receptions for 116 yards.

15. The Chicago Bears and Detroit Lions. The Lions had a 9-2 record entering the game, while the Bears were 8-2-1. Two weeks earlier, the Lions had pounded the Bears 42–10 in

Detroit. The season finale was played on December 16 at Wrigley Field in Chicago. The Bears took a 3–0 first-quarter lead on a 37-yard field goal by George Blanda. In the second quarter, the Lions forged ahead 7–3 on an 18-yard touchdown pass from Harry Gilmer to Bill Bowman. Later in the quarter, Rick Casares raced 68 yards for a touchdown to put the Bears back on top 10–7. By halftime, the score was 17–7. After the Lions cut their deficit to 17–14 in the third quarter, the Bears exploded. Ed Brown threw a 44-yard touchdown pass to Harlon Hill to increase their lead to 24–14 after three quarters. Bobby Watkins scored on a 7-yard touchdown run to make it 31–14, and then Joe Fortunato returned an interception 27 yards for a touchdown for the icing on the cake in what turned out to be a 38–21 Chicago victory.

In the NFL Championship game, the Bears took on the New York Giants, who won the Eastern Conference with an 8-3-1 record. The game was played on December 30 before 56,836 fans at Yankee Stadium in New York. The Giants dominated from the start. A 17-yard touchdown run by Mel Triplett and 2 field goals by Ben Agajanian gave them a 13–0 lead after one quarter. Two short touchdown runs by Alex Webster and a touchdown off a blocked punt by Henry Moore gave New York a 34–7 halftime lead. Kyle Rote caught a 9-yard touchdown pass from Charlie Conerly to up the Giants' lead to 41–7 after three quarters. Conerly completed a 14-yard touchdown pass to Frank Gifford for the game's final points in a 48–7 Giants' rout.

16. Jim Brown. Brown won the NFL rushing crown 8 times, including his rookie season. That year, he ran for a then-record 237 yards against Los Angeles. In the next four seasons, his rushing yardage totals were 1,527, 1,329, 1,257, and 1,408. In November 1, 1959, he set an NFL record that has since been tied with 5 rushing touchdowns against the Baltimore Colts. After a drop-off season in 1962, Brown rushed for a career-high 1,863 yards in 1963. He ran for 1,446 yards in

Jim Brown gets tackled by the New York Giants.
Jerry Coli/Dreamstime.com

1964, a year in which the Browns won the league title. In his final season of 1965, he rushed for 1,544 yards.

Brown never missed a game. Overall, he had 2,359 rushes for 12,312 yards, averaging a remarkable 104.3 yards per game, still an NFL record, and an equally amazing 5.2 yards per carry. He rushed for 106 touchdowns. He had 262 receptions for 2,499 yards with 20 touchdowns. He was a Pro Bowler in all nine seasons and was inducted into the Pro Football Hall of Fame in 1971.

17. The Detroit Lions and San Francisco 49ers. The playoff game was contested on December 22 in front of 60,118 fans at Kezar Stadium in San Francisco. The 49ers took a 14–0 lead after one quarter on long touchdown passes from Y. A. Tittle to R. C. Owens and Hugh McElhenny. After the Lions cut their deficit to 14–7 on a short touchdown pass from Tobin Rote to Steve Junker, the 49ers increased their lead to 24–7 at the half on a 12-yard touchdown pass from Tittle to Billy Wilson and a 25-yard field goal by Gordie Soltau. With the 'Niners leading 27–7, the Lions began what would turn out to be a remarkable comeback. Tom Tracy had touchdown runs of 1 and 58 yards to cut the San Francisco lead to 27–21 after three quarters. In the fourth quarter, Gene Gedman scored from 2 yards out as Detroit forged ahead 28–27. The Lions got some insurance in the form of a 13-yard field goal by Jim Martin en route to a 31–27 triumph.

The Lions' opponent in the NFL Championship game was the Cleveland Browns, who won the Eastern Conference with a 9-2-1 record. The game was played on December 29 before 55,263 fans at Briggs Stadium in Detroit. The Lions won in a rout 59–14.

Rote was 12-of-19 for 280 yards with four touchdowns. Junker had 5 receptions for 109 yards with 2 touchdowns, and Jim Doran had 3 catches for 101 yards, including a 78-yarder for a touchdown from Rote. Cleveland's Milt Plum ran the ball 3 times for 46 yards. Lew Carpenter

rushed the ball 14 times for 82 yards with a touchdown.
A rookie by the name of Jim Brown had 20 carries for 69
yards with a touchdown, and Pete Brewster had 3 receptions for 52 yards.

18. c. 23–17. The Colts finished with a record of 9-3 in winning the Western Conference Championship. The Giants
had a rougher road to the title game. They had to beat the
Browns in the regular-season finale at Yankee Stadium in
New York just to finish in a first-place tie with them at 9-3
in the Eastern Conference. The Giants won that game on a
late 49-yard field goal by Pat Summerall through the high
winds and driving snow. The Giants won the playoff a week
later in the same venue by a 10–0 score.

That set up the duel between the Giants and Colts in the
league title game before 64,185 fans. Summerall's 36-yard
field goal gave New York a 3–0 lead after one quarter. Alan
Ameche's 2-yard touchdown run put Baltimore ahead 7–3
in the second quarter. John Unitas completed a 15-yard
touchdown pass to Raymond Berry to make the score 14–3
at halftime. Mel Triplett scored on a 1-yard run as the Giants
pulled to within 14–10 after three quarters. Frank Gifford
caught a 15-yard touchdown pass from Charlie Conerly to
put the Giants ahead 17–14. The Colts forced overtime on
a 20-yard field goal by Steve Myhra. Ameche scored on a
1-yard touchdown run with 6:45 left in the extra period to
win the game for the Colts.

During overtime, when the Colts were on the 8-yard line
of the Giants on the winning drive, someone ran onto the
field, causing the game to be delayed. According to rumors,
the person who ran onto the field was actually an NBC em-
ployee who was ordered to create a distraction because the
national television feed had gone dead. The difficulty was
the result of an unplugged TV signal cable, and the delay
in the game bought NBC enough time to fix the problem
before the next play.

It was the last time the NFL Championship game had gone to overtime until Super Bowl LI, when the New England Patriots defeated the Atlanta Falcons.

19. b. Jim Brown. The Cleveland Browns' fullback achieved the feat in a 38–31 victory over the Colts before 57,557 fans at Memorial Stadium in Baltimore. Brown ran for a 70-yard touchdown in the second quarter to give Cleveland a 10–3 lead. He scored on a 17-yard run that gave the visitors a 17–10 halftime lead. He had a 3-yard touchdown run in the third quarter to make it 24–10. He scored from a yard out to give his team a 31–17 lead entering the fourth quarter. He had a 1-yard touchdown run for his last score. Overall, he rushed for 172 yards on 32 carries. Brown's feat has been matched three times.

20. True. The Giants finished 10-2 and won the Eastern Conference with ease. The Colts were 9-3 and won the Western Conference by a game over the Chicago Bears. The championship contest was played on December 27 in front of 57,545 fans at Memorial Stadium in Baltimore. Three Pat Summerall field goals and a 60-yard touchdown pass from John Unitas to Lenny Moore made for a 9–7 Giants' lead entering the fourth quarter. That's when Baltimore exploded. Unitas had a 4-yard touchdown run as the Colts forged ahead 14–9. He threw a 12-yard scoring strike to Jerry Richardson to make it 21–9. The dagger to the Giants' heart occurred when Johnny Sample returned an interception 42 yards for a touchdown and a 28–9 Baltimore advantage. The final score was 31–16.

Unitas was 18-of-29 for 264 yards. Moore had 3 receptions for 126 yards, including a 59-yarder from Unitas. Raymond Berry had 5 receptions for 68 yards, including a 28-yarder from Unitas. The Giants' Charlie Conerly was 17-of-37 for 226 yards with a touchdown. Frank Gifford had 8 rushes for 56 yards, while Bob Schnelker had 9 catches for 175 yards, including a 32-yarder for a touchdown from Conerly.

THE 1960s

A NEW LEAGUE AND SUPER BOWLS

The 1960s brought a viable competitor to the NFL—the American Football League. The AFL was different from other professional leagues throughout the years that attempted to challenge the established NFL, most recently the All-America Football Conference from 1946 through 1949. The AFL was a more wide-open, offensive-oriented league than the NFL. Not only did it implement the two-point conversion, it had explosive teams during its ten-year run, like the San Diego Chargers, the Oakland Raiders, and the Kansas City Chiefs. There were great offensive players like George Blanda, Otis Taylor, and, of course, Joe Namath. Beginning with the 1966 season, the NFL champion faced the AFL titlist in what would eventually be called the "Super Bowl," a game that is still played at a predetermined site.

QUESTIONS

1. What Pennsylvania team won the 1960 NFL Championship? *Answer on page 90.*

2. Who were the original eight teams in the AFL in 1960? *Answer on page 91.*

3. The Green Bay Packers defeated the _____ in both the 1961 and 1962 NFL Championship games. *Answer on page 92.*

4. What two teams played in the 1962 AFL Championship game, the third-longest game in pro football history? *Answer on page 93.*

5. What two teams finished in a tie for first place with 7-6-1 records in the AFL Eastern Division in 1963? *Answer on page 93.*

6. What quarterback led the NFL with 3,481 passing yards in 1963? *Answer on page 95.*

  a. John Unitas
  b. Y. A. Tittle
  c. Frank Ryan
  d. Bart Starr

7. Who were the original members of the Los Angeles Rams' "Fearsome Foursome" defense? *Answer on page 95.*

8. Who quarterbacked the Cleveland Browns to the 1964 NFL Championship? *Answer on page 96.*

9. The Cleveland Browns upset the _____ in the 1964 NFL Championship game. *Answer on page 98.*

10. What future politician with the initials J.K. quarterbacked the Buffalo Bills to AFL Championships in 1964 and 1965? *Answer on page 98.*

11. What two teams tied for first place with 10-3-1 records in the 1965 NFL Western Conference? *Answer on page 99.*

12. What two teams played in Super Bowl I? *Answer on page 100.*

13. Who was the first quarterback to pass for 4,000 yards in one season? He achieved the feat in 1967. *Answer on page 101.*

14. In 1967, the NFL switched from just the Eastern Conference and Western Conference to four divisions—two in each conference. What were the names of the four divisions, and what teams were in each division? *Answer on page 102.*

15. What two teams played in the "Ice Bowl" on December 31, 1967? *Answer on page 103.*

16. The Oakland Raiders defeated the New York Jets in the "*Heidi* Game" on November 17, 1968, at the Oakland-Alameda County Coliseum. What was the final score? *Answer on page 104.*

   a. 35–27
   b. 41–36
   c. 31–23
   d. 43–32

17. The Cleveland Browns lost consecutive NFL Championship games in 1968 to the Baltimore Colts and in 1969 to the Los Angeles Rams. True or false? *Answer on page 106.*

18. From where did Joe Namath offer his famous "guarantee" that his New York Jets would upset the Baltimore Colts in Super Bowl III? *Answer on page 107.*

   a. Hotel pool
   b. Miami Touchdown Club
   c. Nightclub
   d. Limousine

19. Who did the Kansas City Chiefs play in Super Bowl IV? *Answer on page 108.*

20. What two Chicago Bears players are on the Team of the Sixties? *Answer on page 109.*

ANSWERS

1. The Philadelphia Eagles. The Eagles finished 10-2 and won the Eastern Conference title, dethroning the two-time defending champion New York Giants. After losing to the Cleveland Browns in their opening game of the season on September 25, the Eagles reeled off nine straight wins, including back-to-back victories over the Giants in late November by scores of 17–10 and 31–23, respectively. In the second of those games, on November 27 at Franklin Field in Philadelphia, the Giants got off to a great start. They took a 14–0 first-quarter lead on 71- and 11-yard touchdown passes from George Shaw to Kyle Rote. Down 17–3 in the second quarter, the Eagles began their comeback. First, Norm Van

Brocklin threw a 25-yard touchdown pass to Ted Dean to pull them within 17–10. They tied the score when J. D. Smith recovered an offensive fumble in the end zone. Trailing 23–17 in the fourth quarter, the Eagles took their first lead, 24–23, when Dean caught a 49-yard touchdown pass from Van Brocklin. The game's final points came when Van Brocklin completed an 8-yard touchdown pass to Billy Ray Barnes. The Eagles lost 27–21 to the Steelers in Pittsburgh on December 11 before concluding the season with a 38–28 win over the Redskins in Washington.

Philadelphia's opponent in the NFL Championship game was the Green Bay Packers, who won the Western Conference with an 8-4 record. In that game, played at Franklin Field, the Packers were up 6–0 in the second quarter when Van Brocklin threw a 35-yard touchdown pass to Tommy McDonald for a one-point Philadelphia lead. The Eagles were up 10–6 at halftime. In the fourth quarter, the Packers forged ahead 13–10 on a 7-yard touchdown pass from Bart Starr to Max McGee. Dean ran 5 yards for a touchdown that gave the Eagles a 17–13 victory.

2. The following were the final standings that year:

Eastern Division

Team	W	L	T	Pct.
Houston Oilers	10	4	0	.714
New York Titans	7	7	0	.500
Buffalo Bills	5	8	1	.385
Boston Patriots	5	9	0	.357

Western Division

Team	W	L	T	Pct.
Los Angeles Chargers	10	4	0	.714
Dallas Texans	8	6	0	.571
Oakland Raiders	6	8	0	.429
Denver Broncos	4	9	1	.308

Houston and Los Angeles played in the AFL title game on New Year's Day 1961 at Jeppesen Stadium in Houston. The Chargers took a 6–0 lead after one quarter on 2 Ben Agajanian field goals. In the second quarter, the Oilers forged ahead 7–6 when George Blanda completed a 17-yard touchdown pass to Dave Smith. At halftime, they led 10–9. In the third quarter, Blanda threw a 7-yard touchdown pass to Bill Groman for a 17–9 Houston advantage. Paul Lowe scored on a short touchdown run to pull Los Angeles to within one point after three quarters, but Blanda threw an 88-yard touchdown strike to Billy Cannon for the game's final points in a 24–16 Oilers win.

Blanda was 16-of-31 for 301 yards. Cannon had 3 receptions for 128 yards and 18 rushes for 50 yards, while Smith had 5 catches for 52 yards and 19 carries for 45 yards. Charley Hennigan caught 4 passes for 71 yards, including a 38-yarder, and Groman had 3 receptions for 37 yards.

For the Chargers, Jack Kemp was 21-of-41 for 171 yards with 2 interceptions. Lowe rushed the ball 21 times for 165 yards. Dave Kocourek had 3 receptions for 57 yards, including a 33-yarder, while Don Norton had 6 catches for 55 yards.

3. New York Giants. In 1961, the Giants finished 10-3-1 in winning the Eastern Conference title, while the Packers were 11-3 in winning the Western Conference crown. In the championship game, played on New Year's Eve at New City Stadium in Green Bay, after a scoreless first quarter, it was all Packers. Paul Hornung gave Green Bay a 7–0 second-quarter lead when he had a 6-yard touchdown run. Then Bart Starr threw touchdown passes to Boyd Dowler and Ron Kramer for a 21–0 Packers' lead. With the score 27–0 in the third quarter, Kramer caught a 13-yard touchdown pass from Starr to increase the lead to 34–0. Hornung's third field goal of the day gave Green Bay a 37–0 victory.

In 1962, the Giants won the Eastern Conference Championship with a 12-2 record, while the Packers took the Western Conference crown with a 13-1 mark. In the title game, played on December 30 at Yankee Stadium in New York, the Packers took a 3–0 lead after one quarter when Jerry Kramer kicked a 26-yard field goal. Jim Taylor's 7-yard touchdown run upped the Green Bay lead to 10–0 at halftime. The Giants cut their deficit to 10–7 in the third quarter when Jim Collier recovered a fumble for a touchdown on the special teams. Jerry Kramer booted 29- and 30-yard field goals in the third and fourth quarters, respectively, for the game's final points in a 16–7 Packers' triumph.

4. The Houston Oilers and Dallas Texans. Both teams finished 11-3 during the regular season, the Oilers winning the Eastern Division and the Texans winning the Western Division. The title game was played on December 23 at Jeppesen Stadium in Houston. The Texans took a 3–0 first-quarter lead on a 16-yard field goal by Tommy Brooker. In the second quarter, Abner Haynes caught a 28-yard touchdown pass from Len Dawson to up the lead to 10–0. Then Haynes had a 2-yard touchdown run to increase the Dallas lead to 17–0 at halftime. In the third quarter, George Blanda threw a 15-yard touchdown pass to Willard Dewveall to cut the Oilers' deficit to 17–7. In the fourth quarter, Blanda kicked a 31-yard field goal to make it 17–10. The Oilers tied the score when Charley "The Human Bowling Ball" Tolar scored from a yard out. With the clock running down, Dave Grayson blocked a 42-yard field-goal attempt by Blanda to end any more scoring threats.

The game went into overtime, but neither team scored in the first extra session. In the second overtime, Jack Spikes picked up 10 yards on a catch from Dawson and then 19 yards on a run. A few plays later, Brooker booted a 25-yard field goal 2:54 into the sixth quarter as the Texans prevailed 20–17 in their last game before moving north to become the Kansas City Chiefs.

5. The Boston Patriots and Buffalo Bills. The two teams tangled in a playoff on December 28 at War Memorial Stadium

in Buffalo. The Patriots took a 10–0 lead after one quarter on a 28-yard field goal by Gino Cappelletti and a 59-yard touchdown pass from Babe Parilli to Larry Garron. Two Cappelletti field goals increased the Boston lead to 16–0 at halftime. Daryle Lamonica completed a 93-yard touchdown pass to Elbert Dubenion to pull Buffalo within 16–8 after three quarters. Parilli and Garron hooked up again, this time on a 17-yard touchdown pass, as the Patriots went up 23–8 en route to a 26–8 victory.

Boston's opponent in the AFL Championship game was the San Diego Chargers, who won the Western Division with an 11-3 record. The title game, played on January 5, 1964, at Balboa Stadium in San Diego, was all Chargers from the beginning. The home team took a 7–0 first-quarter lead on a short touchdown run by Tobin Rote. A 7-yard touchdown run by Garron was sandwiched by long touchdown runs from Keith Lincoln and Paul Lowe for a 21–7 Chargers' lead after the first quarter. With the score 31–10 in the third quarter, Rote fired a 48-yard touchdown pass to Lance Alworth to increase the lead to 38–10. In the fourth quarter, John Hadl threw a 25-yard touchdown pass to Lincoln, and then Hadl scored himself from a yard out for the game's final points in San Diego's 51–10 rout.

The Chargers totaled 610 yards to the Patriots' 261. Rote was 10-of-15 for 173 yards with 2 touchdowns. Hadl was 7-of-11 for 132 yards. Lincoln had 13 rushes for 206 yards and 7 receptions for 123 yards, including a 32-yarder, while Lowe ran the ball 12 times for 94 yards. Alworth had 4 catches for 77 yards, Jacque MacKinnon caught 2 passes for 53 yards, including a 33-yarder, and Don Norton had 2 receptions for 44 yards, including a 30-yarder, with 1 touchdown.

Parilli was 14-of-29 for 189 yards with an interception. Cappelletti had 2 receptions for 72 yards, including a 49-yarder from Parilli, while Art Graham had 2 catches for 68 yards, including a 45-yarder from Parilli.

6. a. John Unitas. That year with the Baltimore Colts, Unitas was 237-of-410 with 20 touchdowns and 12 interceptions. He played for Baltimore from 1956 through 1972. He spent 1973 with the San Diego Chargers. In 1958, he was 136-of-263 for 2,007 yards with 19 touchdowns and 7 interceptions in helping the Colts to a 9-3 record and the Western Conference Championship. In a 23–17 overtime win against the New York Giants in the NFL title game, he was 26-of-40 for 349 yards with a touchdown and an interception.

The next year, Unitas was 193-of-367 for 2,899 yards with 32 touchdowns and 14 picks in leading Baltimore to a 9-3 record and another Western Conference title. In a 31–16 victory over the Giants in the league championship game, he was 18-of-29 for 264 yards with 2 touchdowns. In 1964, he was 158-of-305 for 2,824 yards with 19 touchdowns and 6 interceptions in leading the Colts to a 12-2 record and an appearance in the NFL title game. His last hurrah was in 1970, when he was 166-of-321 for 2,213 yards with 14 touchdowns and 18 interceptions in leading Baltimore to an 11-2-1 record and helping them to a 16–13 victory over the Dallas Cowboys in Super Bowl V.

Overall, Unitas completed 2,830 of 5,186 passes for 40,239 yards with 290 touchdowns and 253 interceptions. He was picked for the Pro Bowl from 1957 through 1964 and in 1966 and 1967. He was inducted into the Pro Football Hall of Fame in 1979.

7. Deacon Jones, Merlin Olsen, Rosey Grier, and Lamar Lundy. Grier left the New York Giants to join Jones, Olsen, and Lundy with Los Angeles in 1963. Their defensive prowess soon earned them their nickname. Jones was the left defensive end, Lundy was the right defensive end, Olsen was the left defensive tackle, and Grier was the right defensive tackle. Chicago Bears linebacker Dick Butkus called them "the most dominant line in football history." They gained fame as the Rams went from a perennial patsy to an NFL powerhouse under head coach George Allen. Roger Brown replaced Grier

in 1967. The Rams' records from 1967 through 1969 were 11-1-2, 10-3-1, and 11-3. Twice during that period, they qualified for the playoffs.

Diron Talbert replaced Brown in 1970. Also in 1970, Coy Bacon replaced Lundy. The line was ultimately broken up when Allen became head coach of the Washington Redskins in 1971. Talbert and Jones, a Pro Football Hall of Famer, left in 1972, with Talbert following Allen to the Redskins, and Jones going to the San Diego Chargers for two years before eventually reuniting with Allen himself on the Redskins in 1974. Bacon left in 1973.

After missing the playoffs from 1970 through 1972, the Rams won seven straight division titles from 1973 through 1979, which was an NFL record until 2016 when broken by the New England Patriots. Those Rams teams were led in part by a reconstituted Fearsome Foursome. This line consisted of ends Jack Youngblood and Fred Dryer and tackles Olsen and Larry Brooks. Youngblood and Olsen are Pro Football Hall of Famers, while Brooks made the Pro Bowl five times. Dryer, acquired from the Giants in 1972, made the Pro Bowl once and set an NFL record with 2 safeties in one game—both in the fourth quarter!—during a 24–7 victory over the Green Bay Packers on October 21, 1973. Olsen, who played with his brother Phil Olsen, a defensive tackle, for four seasons from 1971 through 1974, retired after a fifteen-year career following the 1976 season. He was replaced by Mike Fanning.

8. Frank Ryan. In that 1964 season, he was 174-of-334 for 2,404 yards with an NFL-best 25 touchdowns and 19 interceptions as the Browns won the Eastern Conference title with a 10-3-1 record. He threw three second-half touchdown passes—for 18, 42, and 51 yards—to Gary Collins then led Cleveland to a 27–0 upset of Baltimore in the NFL Championship game.

Ryan was traded to the Browns from Los Angeles on July 12, 1962. After sharing the signal-calling duties with Jim

The LA Rams' Merlin Olsen tries to get a hand on the NY Jets' Joe Namath.
Jerry Coli/Dreamstime.com

Ninowski that year, in 1963 he was the starter and went 135-of-256 for 2,026 yards with 25 touchdowns and 13 interceptions in directing the Browns to a 10-4 record and second-place finish in the Eastern Conference. Two years later, he played a big part in the team returning to the title game, but the Browns lost to Green Bay. In 1966, he passed for 2,974 yards with a league-high 29 touchdowns and only 14 interceptions. He helped Cleveland to a 9-5 record and the Century Division title in 1967. He was replaced by Bill Nelsen three games into the 1968 season.

Ryan was released on September 9, 1969, some two weeks before the start of the season. He was a backup with Washington that year and the following season. Overall, he completed 1,090 of 2,133 passes for 16,042 yards with 149 touchdowns and 111 interceptions. He was a Pro Bowler from 1964 through 1966.

9. Baltimore Colts. The game was played at Cleveland Municipal Stadium on December 27 before 79,544 fans. The Browns, who won the Eastern Conference with a 10-3-1 record, were heavy underdogs to the John Unitas–led Colts, who easily won the Western Conference with a 12-2 record. The Browns broke a scoreless tie in the third quarter on a 43-yard field goal by Lou Groza. Later in the third, Frank Ryan threw an 18-yard touchdown pass to Gary Collins to make it 10–0. Ryan hit Collins again on a 42-yard touchdown pass for a 17–0 lead after three quarters. Groza's 10-yard field goal upped the Cleveland lead to 20–0. Ryan connected with Collins again on a 51-yard touchdown pass for the final points of the game in the Browns' 27–0 victory.

10. Jack Kemp. Kemp would eventually become a member of the U.S. House of Representatives, Chair of the House Republican Conference, and the ninth U.S. Secretary of Housing and Urban Development. But he had football business to take care of first. He began his pro football career with the Pittsburgh Steelers in 1957. He had two successful seasons with the Chargers in 1960 and 1961, leading the 1961

team to the AFL Championship game. He joined Buffalo during the 1962 season.

After the Bills finished 7-6-1 in 1963, Kemp led them in 1964 to a 12-2 record and the Eastern Division title. The Bills played Kemp's old team, the Western Division champion San Diego Chargers, in the AFL title game on December 26 at War Memorial Stadium in Buffalo. The Chargers took a 7–0 first-quarter lead on a 26-yard touchdown pass from Tobin Rote to Dave Kocourek. A short field goal by Pete Gogolak cut the Bills' deficit to 7–3 after one quarter. The Bills took a 10–7 lead in the second quarter on a 4-yard touchdown run by Wray Carlton. Gogolak knocked home a 17-yard field goal to up the Buffalo lead to 13–7 at the half. Kemp scored from a yard out in the fourth quarter for the game's final points in a 20–7 Bills' victory.

The next year, Buffalo won the weak Eastern Division again with a 10-3-1 record. Its opponent in the league championship game was, once again, the Chargers, who won the Western Division with a 9-2-3 record. The game was played on December 26, this time at Balboa Stadium in San Diego. It didn't matter. After a scoreless first quarter, the Bills dominated. In the second quarter, Kemp threw an 18-yard touchdown pass to Ernie Warlick for a 7–0 Buffalo lead. Later in the quarter, Butch Byrd returned an interception 74 yards for a touchdown and a 14–0 Bills' halftime lead. Three Gogolak field goals in the second half gave Buffalo a 23–0 triumph.

11. The Green Bay Packers and Baltimore Colts. How the tie happened was beyond belief. Heading into the final weekend of the regular season, the Packers had a record of 10-3. The Colts were 9-3-1. The Colts needed to beat the Rams in Los Angeles on Saturday, December 18, and, the next day, have the Packers tie or lose to the 49ers in San Francisco. The Colts beat the Rams 20–17 and, believe it or not, the favored Packers were tied by the 49ers 24–24, leaving both Baltimore and Green Bay with 10-3-1 records. The

two teams tangled in a playoff on December 26 at Lambeau Field in Green Bay for the right to face the defending NFL champion—and Eastern Conference titlist—Cleveland Browns in the league championship game.

In the playoff game, the Colts took a 7–0 first-quarter lead when Don Shinnick returned a fumble 25 yards for a touchdown. Their lead grew to 10–0 at halftime on Shinnick's 15-yard field goal in the second quarter. The Packers cut their deficit to 10–7 after three quarters when Paul Hornung scored from a yard out. Don Chandler's 22-yard field goal tied the game 10–10. There were many Colts fans who believed the kick sailed high and wide. But it was to no avail, and overtime was next. Chandler's 25-yard field goal with 1:21 to go accounted for the winning points in Green Bay's 13–10 victory.

The championship game between the Packers and Browns was played on January 2, 1966, at Lambeau Field. A massive snowstorm had hit Green Bay the night before, forcing the Browns and Packers to played in a mud bath. The Packers took a 7–0 lead in the first quarter when Bart Starr threw a 47-yard touchdown pass to Carroll Dale. The Browns pulled to within 7–6 on a 17-yard touchdown pass from Frank Ryan to Gary Collins. They took a 9–7 lead after one quarter when Lou Groza kicked a 24-yard field goal. Two field goals by Chandler and another by Groza left the Packers with a 13–12 halftime lead. In the third quarter, Hornung had a 13-yard touchdown run to increase the Green Bay lead to 20–12. Chandler's 29-yard field goal in the fourth quarter was the game's final points in the Packers' 23–12 triumph.

12. The Green Bay Packers and the Kansas City Chiefs. The Packers finished 12–2 in winning the NFL Western Conference title. They defeated the Dallas Cowboys 34–27 in the "Ice Bowl" league championship game. The Chiefs were 11-2-1 and were AFL Western Division champions. They beat the Buffalo Bills 31–7 in the league title game.

Super Bowl I was played on January 15, 1967, at the Los Angeles Memorial Coliseum before just 61,946 fans (many fans were not sold yet on the two leagues' champions playing one another). The Packers took a 7–0 first-quarter lead when Bart Starr completed a 37-yard touchdown pass to Max McGee. The Chiefs tied the score in the second quarter on a 7-yard touchdown pass from Len Dawson to Curtis McClinton. Later in the quarter, Jim Taylor's 14-yard touchdown run upped the Green Bay lead to 14–7. Mike Mercer's 31-yard field goal cut the Packers' lead to 14–10 at halftime. In the third quarter, Elijah Pitts had a 5-yard touchdown run to up the lead to 21–10. McGee caught a 13-yard touchdown pass from Starr to make it 28–10 after three quarters. Pitts scored on a 1-yard run for the game's final points in Green Bay's 35–10 win.

Starr was 16-of-23 for 250 yards with an interception. Taylor had 17 rushes for 56 yards, while Pitts ran the ball 11 times for 45 yards and had 2 receptions for 32 yards. Donny Anderson had 4 carries for 30 yards. McGee had 7 catches for 138 yards, and Carroll Dale caught 4 passes for 59 yards, including a 25-yarder.

Dawson was 16-of-27 for 211 yards with an interception. He ran the ball 3 times for 24 yards. Chris Buford had 4 receptions for 67 yards, including a 27-yarder. Otis Taylor had 4 catches for 57 yards, including a 31-yarder. McClinton caught 2 passes for 34 yards, including a 27-yarder, while Fred Arbanas had 2 receptions for 30 yards. Mike Garrett had 3 catches for 28 yards.

13. Joe Namath. "Broadway Joe" did it in 1967 when he threw for 4,007 yards in helping the New York Jets to an 8-5-1 record and second-place standing in the AFL Eastern Division. In a Week 2 38–24 victory over the Broncos in Denver that season, Namath was 22-of-37 for 399 yards with 2 touchdowns and 2 interceptions. He threw 31- and 3-yard touchdown passes to George Sauer and Mark Smolinski, respectively. The next week, in a 29–7 home win over the Miami Dolphins, Namath

was 23-of-39 for 415 yards with 3 touchdowns and an interception, his only 400-yard game of the season. All of his touchdown passes came in the second half—49- and 5-yarders to Emerson Boozer and a 13-yarder to Smolinski.

In a 30–23 win at home over the Boston Patriots on October 29, Namath was 22-of-43 for 362 yards with 2 touchdowns and 2 picks. His touchdown passes were short ones to Bill Mathis and Pete Lammons. In a 38–29 loss to the Raiders in Oakland on December 17, he was 27-of-46 for 370 yards with 3 touchdowns and 3 interceptions. His touchdown passes were to Don Maynard (28 yards, 5 yards) and Sauer (24 yards). Namath also scored from a yard out after recovering one of his teammate's fumbles. He closed the season with perhaps his finest performance of the year, going 18-of-26 for 343 yards with 4 touchdowns in a 42–32 victory over the Chargers in San Diego. His touchdown passes were to Maynard (13 yards, 26 yards, 36 yards) and Sauer (36 yards).

Overall that year, Namath was 258-of-491 with 26 touchdowns and 28 interceptions.

14. The following were the final standings that season:

Eastern Conference
Capitol Division

Team	W	L	T	Pct.
Dallas Cowboys	9	5	0	.643
Philadelphia Eagles	6	7	1	.462
Washington Redskins	5	6	3	.455
New Orleans Saints	3	11	0	.214

Century Division

Team	W	L	T	Pct.
Cleveland Browns	9	5	0	.643
New York Giants	7	7	0	.500
St. Louis Cardinals	6	7	1	.462
Pittsburgh Steelers	4	9	1	.308

Western Conference
Coastal Division

Team	W	L	T	Pct.
Los Angeles Rams	11	1	2	.917
Baltimore Colts	11	1	2	.917
San Francisco 49ers	7	7	0	.500
Atlanta Falcons	1	12	1	.077

Central Division

Team	W	L	T	Pct.
Green Bay Packers	9	4	1	.692
Chicago Bears	7	6	1	.538
Detroit Lions	5	7	2	.417
Minnesota Vikings	3	8	3	.273

15. The Dallas Cowboys and the Green Bay Packers. It was the NFL Championship game played at Lambeau Field in Green Bay. Dallas finished 9-5 in winning the Capitol Division and routed the Cleveland Browns in the Eastern Conference Championship game. Green Bay was 9-4-1 in winning the Central Division and beat the Los Angeles Rams in the Western Conference title tilt.

The NFL Championship game was played in minus fifteen-degree weather that, with the wind chill factor, felt like forty-eight degrees below zero. Prior to the game, many of the Green Bay players were unable to start their cars in the freezing weather, forcing them to make alternate travel arrangements to make it to the stadium on time. Dave Robinson had to flag down a random passing motorist for a ride!

The referees for the game found they did not have sufficient clothing for the cold, and had to make an early trip to a sporting goods store for earmuffs, heavy gloves, and thermal underwear. The officials were unable to use their whistles after the opening kickoff. As Norm Schachter blew his metal whistle to signal the start of play, it froze to his lips. As he attempted to free the whistle from his lips, the skin ripped off and his lips began to bleed. The conditions were so hostile that, instead of forming a scab, the blood simply froze to his lip. For the rest of the game, the officials used voice commands and calls to end plays and officiate the game.

As for the game itself, the Packers took a 14–0 lead on touchdown passes from Starr to Boyd Dowler, an 8-yarder in the first quarter and a 46-yarder in the second quarter. The Cowboys cut their deficit in half when George Andrie returned a fumble 7 yards for a touchdown. They made it 14–10 at halftime on a 21-yard field goal by Danny Villanueva. The Cowboys took a 17–14 lead in the third quarter when Lance Rentzel caught a 50-yard touchdown pass from halfback Dan Reeves. Starr scored from a yard out for the winning points with just seconds remaining in a 21–17 Green Bay victory.

16. d. 43–32. The game was notable for its exciting finish in which Oakland scored 2 touchdowns in the final minute to win the game. It got its name, though, for a decision by the game's television broadcast network, NBC, to break away from its coverage of the game on the East Coast to broadcast the television film *Heidi*, causing many viewers to miss the Raiders' comeback.

Both teams entered the game with 7-2 records. The Jets took a 6–0 first-quarter lead on two Jim Turner field goals. The Raiders took a 7–6 lead after one quarter on a 9-yard touchdown pass from Daryle Lamonica to Warren Wells. In the second quarter, Lamonica hit Billy Cannon on a 48-yard touchdown pass to increase the Oakland lead to 14–6. The Jets came back and pulled to within 14–12 at halftime on a 1-yard touchdown run by Joe Namath. Entering the fourth quarter, the Raiders were up 22–19. Namath completed a 50-yard touchdown pass to Don Maynard as the Jets took a 26–22 lead. A short Turner field goal made it 29–22, but Lamonica threw a 22-yard touchdown pass to Fred Biletnikoff to tie the score 29–29. Turner kicked a 26-yard field goal to give New York a 32–29 lead.

In the late 1960s, few professional football games took longer than two and a half hours to play, and the Jets–Raiders' three-hour time slot was thought to be adequate. A high-scoring contest combined with a number of injuries and penalties for the two bitter AFL rivals caused the game to run long. NBC executives had originally ordered that *Heidi* begin at 7 p.m. Eastern Standard Time, but decided

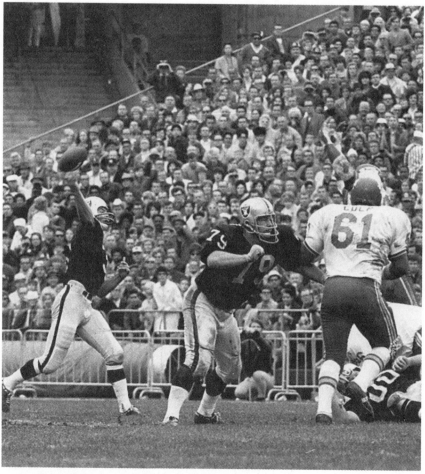

Daryle Lamonica, known as the "Mad Bomber," throws one deep.
Jerry Coli/Dreamstime.com

to allow the game to air to its conclusion. However, as 7 p.m. approached, NBC's switchboards were jammed by viewers phoning to inquire about the night's schedule, preventing the planned change from being communicated. *Heidi* began as scheduled, preempting the final moments of the game and the two Oakland touchdowns in the eastern part of the country, to the outrage of viewers. Those two Raiders scores came on a 43-yard pass from Lamonica to Charlie Smith that gave them a 36–32 lead and, on the ensuing kickoff, a 2-yard fumble return by Preston Ridlehuber for the game's final points.

Response to the preemption by viewers and other critics was negative. The family members of several Jets players were unaware of the game's actual conclusion, while NBC received further criticism for its poor timing in displaying the final score of the game during the *Heidi* movie. NBC's president, Julian Goodman, formally apologized for the incident. In the aftermath, NBC installed special "*Heidi* phones" with a connection to a different telephone exchange from other network phones to ensure that network personnel could communicate under similar circumstances. The game also had an influence on sports broadcasting practices. The future NFL would contractually stipulate that all game telecasts be shown to their conclusion in the markets of the visiting team, while other major leagues and events adopted similar mandates. In 1997, the *Heidi* Game was voted the most memorable regular-season game in pro football history.

17. False. The Browns lost the 1969 league title game to the Minnesota Vikings. In 1968, the Browns finished 10-4, upset the Dallas Cowboys in the Eastern Conference Championship game, but were buried by Baltimore at home 34–0 in the NFL title game. After Lou Michaels gave the Colts a 3–0 second-quarter lead on a 28-yard field goal, Tom Matte had 3 straight touchdown runs—1- and 12-yarders in the second quarter and a 2-yarder in the third quarter—for a 24–0 Baltimore lead entering the fourth period. Michaels

hit a short field goal, and Timmy Brown scored from 4 yards out for the game's final points.

In 1969, the Browns were 10-3-1, shocked the Cowboys again in the conference title game, but were bulldozed 27–7 by the Vikings in the league championship game at Metropolitan Stadium in Minnesota in eight-degree weather that, with the wind chill, made it feel like six below. The frigid air did not seem to bother the Vikings. Joe Kapp scored on a 7-yard touchdown run to give them a 7–0 first-quarter lead. He then threw a 75-yard touchdown pass to Gene Washington to up the home team's lead to 14–0 after one quarter. Fred Cox's 30-yard field goal and Dave Osborn's 20-yard touchdown run gave Minnesota a 24–0 halftime lead. Cox booted a 32-yard field goal in the third quarter to make it 27–0. The Browns finally got on the board in the fourth quarter when Bill Nelsen completed a short touchdown pass to Gary Collins for the game's final points.

18. b. Miami Touchdown Club. The Jets finished 11-3 in 1968 and defeated the Oakland Raiders 27–23 in the AFL Championship game. The Colts were 13-1 and routed the Cleveland Browns 34–0 in the NFL Championship contest. Despite the Jets' accomplishments, AFL teams were generally not regarded as having the same caliber of talent as NFL teams. However, three days before the game, Namath appeared at the Miami Touchdown Club and boldly predicted to the audience, "We're gonna win the game. I guarantee it." Jets head coach Weeb Ewbank, in an NFL Films segment, once joked that he "could have shot" Namath for his statement. Namath made his famous guarantee in response to a rowdy Colts supporter at the club, who boasted that the Colts would easily defeat the Jets. Namath said he never intended to make such a public prediction and never would have done so had he not been confronted by the fan.

Nevertheless, Namath's comments and subsequent performance in the game itself are two of the more famous milestones in NFL lore. He was 17-of-28 for 206 yards, including a 39-yard pass to George Sauer, in leading the Jets to a 16–7 victory. Matt Snell gave them a 7–0 second-quarter lead when he scored from 4 yards out. By the fourth quarter, three Jim Turner field goals had given the Jets a 16–0 lead. Jerry Hill scored a meaningless touchdown from a yard out for the game's final points.

Snell had thirty rushes for 121 yards and 4 receptions for 40 yards. Sauer had 8 catches for 133 yards. For Baltimore, John Unitas was 11-of-24 for 110 yards with an interception. Earl Morrall was 6-of-17 for 71 yards with 3 picks. Tom Matte ran the ball 11 times for 116 yards, including a 58-yarder, and caught 2 passes for 30 yards. Willie Richardson had 6 receptions for 58 yards, Jimmy Orr had 3 catches for 42 yards, and John Mackey caught 3 passes for 35 yards.

19. The Minnesota Vikings. The Chiefs won 23–7 on January 11, 1970, at Tulane Stadium in New Orleans. They finished 11-3 and won the AFL Championship 17–7 over the Oakland Raiders. The Vikings were 12-2 and won the NFL title 27–7 over the Cleveland Browns. The Chiefs featured Len Dawson, Mike Garrett, and Otis Taylor on offense and Willie Lanier, Emmitt Thomas, and Johnny Robinson on defense. The Vikings featured the "Purple People Eaters"— left defensive end Carl Eller, right defensive end Jim Marshall, left defensive tackle Gary Larsen, and right defensive tackle Alan Page.

Three Jan Stenerud field goals gave the Chiefs a 9–0 lead in the second quarter. Garrett had a 5-yard touchdown run to expand the lead to 16–0 at halftime. In the third quarter, Dave Osborn ran for a 4-yard touchdown to cut the Vikings' deficit to 16–7. The Chiefs put the game on ice later in the quarter when Dawson completed a 46-yard touchdown pass to Taylor for the game's final points in a 23–7 Kansas City victory.

Dawson was 12-of-17 for 142 yards with an interception. Garrett had 11 rushes for 39 yards and 2 receptions for

25 yards. Frank Pitts ran the ball 3 times for 37 yards and caught 3 passes for 33 yards. Taylor had 6 catches for 81 yards. For Minnesota, Joe Kapp was 16-of-25 for 183 yards with 2 picks. John Henderson had 7 receptions for 111 yards, including a 28-yarder, while John Beasley caught 2 passes for 41 yards, including a 26-yarder.

20. Gale Sayers and Dick Butkus. Both Sayers and Butkus were drafted by the Bears in 1965—Butkus with the third overall pick out of the University of Illinois and Sayers as the fourth overall choice out of the University of Kansas. Sayers is considered to be one of the greatest running backs who ever lived. In 1965, he had 166 rushes for 867 yards with 14 touchdowns and 29 receptions for 507 yards with 6 touchdowns. On December 12 that year, he tied an NFL record by scoring 6 touchdowns in a 61–20 win over the San Francisco 49ers at Wrigley Field in Chicago—4 on rushes, 1 on a reception, and the last one on an 86-yard punt return. In 1966, Sayers ran the ball 229 times for an NFL-leading 1,231 yards with 8 touchdowns and had 34 receptions for 447 yards with 2 touchdowns. In 1969, he had 236 carries for a league-leading 1,032 yards with 8 touchdowns and had 17 catches for 116 yards. He played with the Bears through 1971.

Overall, Sayers had 991 rushes for 4,956 yards with 39 touchdowns and had 112 receptions for 1,307 yards with 9 touchdowns. He also returned 6 kickoffs for touchdowns and 2 punts for touchdowns. He was a Pro Bowler from 1965 through 1967 and in 1969. He was inducted into the Pro Football Hall of Fame in 1977.

Butkus, a middle linebacker, was known for his ferociousness and nose for the football. He caused havoc for opposing running backs. He had 5 interceptions in 1965, 4 in 1971, and 3 each in 1968 and 1970. Overall, he had 22 interceptions. He had 7 fumble returns in 1965, 4 each in 1966 and 1972, and 3 in both 1967 and 1971. All-time, he had 27 fumble recoveries, including one that he returned for his only touchdown in a 35–14 win over the Houston Oilers on October 28, 1973, in which he was playing in his final season. He was a Pro Bowler from 1965 through 1972 and was enshrined into the Pro Football Hall of Fame in 1979.

Unfortunately for both of them, Sayers and Butkus played on mostly average Bears teams and thus never played in a postseason game.

THE 1970s

MONDAY NIGHT FOOTBALL, MERGERS, AND RIVALRIES

In 1970, the NFL and American Football League merged to become one twenty-six-team National Football League. Two more teams would join the fray later in the decade. With the merger, although old rivalries remained, new rivalries were established. The 1970s also brought the advent of ABC's *Monday Night Football* and, later in the decade, special Thursday night and Sunday night games on the same network.

QUESTIONS

1. What three NFL teams joined the ten AFL teams in the new American Football Conference of the new NFL in 1970? *Answer on page 114.*

   a. Baltimore, Pittsburgh, Miami
   b. Pittsburgh, Chicago, New England

c. Philadelphia, Cleveland, Oakland

d. Baltimore, Cleveland, Pittsburgh

2. I was the third overall pick in the 1970 NFL Draft after Cleveland traded Paul Warfield to Miami for the right to draft me. I had been a quarterback at Purdue University from 1967 through 1969. Who am I? *Answer on page 115.*

3. What two teams played in the first ABC *Monday Night Football* game? *Answer on page 116.*

4. Who set an NFL record with a 63-yard field goal on November 8, 1970? *Answer on page 116.*

5. What two teams played in the longest game ever on Christmas Day 1971? *Answer on page 117.*

6. What two teams played in Super Bowl VI? *Answer on page 118.*

   a. Dallas Cowboys, Oakland Raiders

   b. Washington Redskins, Miami Dolphins

   c. Dallas Cowboys, Miami Dolphins

   d. Los Angeles Rams, Pittsburgh Steelers

7. What two teams played in the "Immaculate Reception" game on December 23, 1972? *Answer on page 120.*

8. What quarterback was nicknamed "Captain Comeback" due to his fourth-quarter game-winning heroics? *Answer on page 121.*

9. What team finished 17-0, including the postseason, in 1972 and won Super Bowl VII? *Answer on page 122.*

10. What team finished 1-13 in both 1972 and 1973? *Answer on page 124.*

   a. Buffalo Bills
   b. San Diego Chargers
   c. Philadelphia Eagles
   d. Houston Oilers

11. In Week 2 of the 1973 season, the Miami Dolphins lost 12–7 to the Oakland Raiders. In what stadium in the State of California was the game played? *Answer on page 124.*

12. What four players who were drafted by the Pittsburgh Steelers in 1974 became Pro Football Hall of Famers and helped the Steelers to four Super Bowl titles in six seasons from 1974 through 1979? *Answer on page 125.*

13. What two teams played in the "Sea of Hands" AFC Divisional Playoff game on December 21, 1974? *Answer on page 126.*

14. In what stadium did a small plane crash just hours after a 1976 playoff game? *Answer on page 127.*

15. What teams played in Super Bowl XI? *Answer on page 128.*

16. The Tampa Bay Buccaneers lost their first _____ games upon joining the NFL in 1976. *Answer on page 129.*

   a. 22
   b. 24
   c. 26
   d. 28

17. What was the Denver "Orange Crush" Broncos' record in 1977? *Answer on page 132.*

18. Who played in "The Mud Bowl" in the 1977 playoffs? *Answer on page 133.*

19. What team did the New York Giants oppose in the "Miracle at the Meadowlands" game on November 19, 1978? *Answer on page 134.*

20. Against what team did Houston Oilers rookie Earl Campbell have his coming-out party with 199 yards rushing on *Monday Night Football* on November 20, 1978? *Answer on page 135.*

ANSWERS

1. d. Baltimore, Cleveland, Pittsburgh. Both the American Football Conference and the National Football Conference had thirteen teams. The following are the final standings that year:

AFC
Eastern Division

Team	W	L	T	Pct.
Baltimore Colts	11	2	1	.846
Miami Dolphins	10	4	0	.714
New York Jets	4	10	0	.286
Buffalo Bills	3	10	1	.231
Boston Patriots	2	12	0	.143

Central Division

Team	W	L	T	Pct.
Cincinnati Bengals	8	6	0	.571
Cleveland Browns	7	7	0	.500
Pittsburgh Steelers	5	9	0	.357
Houston Oilers	3	10	1	.231

Western Division

Team	W	L	T	Pct.
Oakland Raiders	8	4	2	.667
Kansas City Chiefs	5	2		.583
San Diego Chargers	5	6	3	.455
Denver Broncos	5	8	1	.385

NFC

Eastern Division

Team	W	L	T	Pct.
Dallas Cowboys	10	4	0	.714
New York Giants	9	5	0	.643
St. Louis Cardinals	8	5	1	.615
Washington Redskins	6	8	0	.429
Philadelphia Eagles	3	10	1	.231

Central Division

Team	W	L	T	Pct.
Minnesota Vikings	12	2	0	.857
Detroit Lions	10	4	0	.714
Green Bay Packers	6	8	0	.429
Chicago Bears	6	8	0	.429

Western Division

Team	W	L	T	Pct.
San Francisco 49ers	10	3	1	.769
Los Angeles Rams	9	4	1	.692
Atlanta Falcons	4	8	2	.333
New Orleans Saints	2	11	1	.154

2. Mike Phipps. I had directed the Boilermakers to a 24-6 record, including a pair of Associated Press top-ten finishes. I became the Browns' full-time starter in the second week of the 1972 season. That year, I was 144-of-305 for 1,994 yards with 13 touchdowns and 16 interceptions. We went 10-4 and lost to the undefeated Dolphins 20–14 in an AFC Divisional Playoff at the Orange Bowl in Miami.

My touchdown passes/interceptions ratios for the next three seasons were 9/20, 9/17, and 4/19. Our records those years fell to 7-5-2, 4-10, and 3-11, respectively. I suffered a separated shoulder during the 1976 season opener that caused me to miss most of the season. I was traded to Chicago on May 3, 1977. I helped the Bears qualify for the 1979 playoffs. In a 27–17 NFC Wild Card Playoff loss to Philadelphia, I was 13-of-30 for 142 yards with 2 interceptions. I played with the Bears through 1981.

Overall, I completed 886 of 1,799 passes for 10,506 yards with 55 touchdowns and 108 interceptions.

3. The New York Jets and Cleveland Browns. The Browns beat the Jets 31–21 on September 21, 1970, before a Browns home record 85,703 fans at Cleveland Municipal Stadium. After a handful of attempts by the networks of playing games in prime time, this try by ABC was the first real package of games over a period of time. The Browns took a 7–0 lead in the first quarter on an 8-yard touchdown pass from Bill Nelsen to Gary Collins. Bo Scott scored on a 2-yard run later in the quarter to make the score 14–0. The Jets cut the deficit to 14–7 at halftime on a 5-yard touchdown run by Emerson Boozer.

The Browns upped their lead to 21–7 when Homer Jones returned the second-half kickoff 94 yards for a touchdown. Boozer's 10-yard touchdown run later in the third quarter made the score 21–14, but Don Cockroft kicked a 27-yard field goal to give Cleveland a 24–14 lead entering the fourth quarter. Joe Namath hit George Sauer for a 33-yard touchdown to pull New York within 24–21. Billy Andrews clinched the Browns' victory when he dove for an interception of a Namath pass, got up, and returned the ball 25 yards for a touchdown with thirty-five seconds left.

4. Tom Dempsey. The New Orleans kicker gave the Saints a 19–17 win over the Detroit Lions with the last-second kick at Tulane Stadium in New Orleans. Dempsey was born without toes on his right foot and no fingers on his right hand. He wore a modified shoe with a flattened and enlarged toe sur-

face. This generated controversy about whether such a shoe gave a player an unfair advantage. But when an analysis of his kick was carried out by ESPN Sport Science years later, it was found that his modified shoe had offered him no advantage—in fact, it was found that the smaller contact area could have reduced, not increased, the margin for error.

With time running out in the New Orleans–Detroit game, the Saints attempted a field goal with holder Joe Scarpati spotting at their own 37-yard line (this was at a time when the field-goal uprights were located on the goal line). The snap from Jackie Burkett was good, and Dempsey nailed the field goal with a couple of feet to spare. The win was one of only two for the Saints in a dismal season.

With the kick, Dempsey broke Bert Rechichar's seventeen-year-old NFL record for longest field goal by 7 yards. Dempsey's record was equaled by Denver's Jason Elam in 1998, Oakland's Sebastian Janikowski in 2011, and San Francisco's David Akers in 2012 (Carolina's Graham Gano matched the mark on October 7, 2018). On December 8, 2013, the Broncos' Matt Prater topped everyone by hitting a 64-yard field goal in a win over Tennessee.

Dempsey, whose rookie year with the Saints was in 1969, also played for the Philadelphia Eagles, Los Angeles Rams, Houston Oilers, and Buffalo Bills. He never came close to his record-breaking kick. His second-longest field goal was a 55-yarder in his rookie season. He retired after the 1979 season.

5. The Miami Dolphins and Kansas City Chiefs. The Dolphins defeated the Chiefs 27–24 in double overtime in an AFC Divisional Playoff at Municipal Stadium in Kansas City. The game went eighty-two minutes and forty seconds. The Chiefs took a 10–0 lead after one quarter on a Jan Stenerud field goal and a 7-yard touchdown pass from Len Dawson to Ed Podolak. The Dolphins tied the game by halftime on a short touchdown run by Larry Csonka and a short field goal by Garo Yepremian. The teams traded 1-yard touchdown runs

in the third quarter, first by the Chiefs' Jim Otis and the second by the Dolphins' Jim Kiick, resulting in a 17–17 tie entering the fourth quarter. Kansas City took a 24–17 lead on a 3-yard touchdown run by Podolak, but Miami tied the score on a 5-yard touchdown pass from Bob Griese to Marv Fleming. The Dolphins won the game when Yepremian booted a 37-yard field goal seven minutes and forty seconds into the second overtime.

Griese was 20-of-35 for 263 yards with 2 interceptions. Csonka had 24 rushes for 86 yards, including a 29-yarder. Kiick ran the ball 15 times for 56 yards and had 3 receptions for 24 yards. Paul Warfield had 7 catches for 140 yards, including a 35-yarder. Howard Twilley caught 5 passes for 58 yards, including a 23-yarder, while Fleming had 4 receptions for 37 yards.

Dawson was 18-of-26 for 246 yards with 2 picks. Wendell Hayes rushed the ball 22 times for 100 yards. Podolak had 17 carries for 85 yards, including a 32-yarder, and had 8 catches for 110 yards, including a 29-yarder. Elmo Wright caught 3 passes for 104 yards, including a 63-yarder.

6. c. Dallas Cowboys, Miami Dolphins. Miami finished 10-3-1 and won the AFC Championship game 21–0 over the Baltimore Colts. Dallas was 11-3 and defeated the San Francisco 49ers 14–3 in the NFC Championship game. The Super Bowl was played on January 16, 1972, at Tulane Stadium in New Orleans. The Cowboys took a 3–0 first-quarter lead on a 9-yard field goal by Mike Clark. In the second quarter, Roger Staubach threw a 7-yard touchdown pass to Lance Alworth for a 10–0 Dallas lead. Miami cut its deficit to 10–3 by halftime on a 31-yard field goal by Garo Yepremian. In the third quarter, Duane Thomas scored from 3 yards out to increase the Cowboys' lead to 17–3 entering the fourth quarter. Mike Ditka caught a 7-yard touchdown pass from Staubach for the game's final points in a 24–3 Dallas victory.

Staubach was 12-of-19 for 119 yards. Thomas had 19 rushes for 95 yards, and Walt Garrison ran the ball 14 times

Len Dawson running with the football
Jerry Coli/Dreamstime.com

for 74 yards. Alworth and Ditka each had 2 receptions for 28 yards, while Bob Hayes had 2 catches for 23 yards.

Griese was 12-of-23 for 134 yards with an interception. Jim Kiick had 10 rushes for 40 yards and 3 receptions for 21 yards, and Larry Csonka had 9 carries for 40 yards and 2 catches for 18 yards. Paul Warfield caught 4 passes for 39 yards, while Marv Fleming and Howard Twilley each caught a single pass—Fleming's for 27 yards and Twilley's for 20 yards.

7. The Oakland Raiders and Pittsburgh Steelers. The Raiders finished 10-3-1 during the regular season and won the AFC Western Division title. The Steelers were 11-3 and won the AFC Central Division title. This divisional playoff game was played in front of 50,350 fans at Three Rivers Stadium in Pittsburgh. After a scoreless first half, the Steelers took a 3–0 third-quarter lead when Roy Gerela kicked an 18-yard field goal. He booted a 29-yard field goal in the fourth quarter for a 6–0 Pittsburgh lead. The Raiders took a 7–6 lead when Ken Stabler raced 30 yards down the left sideline for a touchdown with one minute and seventeen seconds to go.

On fourth-and-ten at their own 40-yard line with twenty-two seconds remaining and no time-outs left, Pittsburgh head coach Chuck Noll called a pass play, 66 Circle Option, intended for receiver Barry Pearson, a rookie who was playing in his very first NFL game. Terry Bradshaw, though, under great pressure from Raiders linemen Tony Cline and Horace Jones, threw the ball to the Raiders' 35-yard line toward halfback John "Frenchy" Fuqua. Safety Jack Tatum collided with Fuqua just as the ball arrived. Tatum's hit knocked Fuqua to the ground and sent the ball sailing backward several yards, end over end.

Fullback Franco Harris, after initially blocking on the play, had run downfield in case Bradshaw needed another eligible receiver. He scooped up the sailing ball just before it hit the ground. He ran past linebacker Gerald Irons, while linebacker Phil Villapiano, who had been covering Harris, was blocked by tight end John McMakin. Harris used a stiff-arm to ward off defensive back Jimmy Warren and went in for a touchdown, thus the Immaculate Reception.

Or was it *not* a touchdown?

The critical question was: Who did the football touch in the Fuqua/Tatum collision? If it bounced off Fuqua without ever touching Tatum, then Harris's reception was illegal. If the ball bounced off only Tatum, or if it bounced off both Fuqua and Tatum (in any order), then the reception was legal. The rule stated in the pertinent part that, once an offensive player touches a pass, he is the only offensive player eligible to catch the pass. However, if a [defensive] player touches [the] pass first, or simultaneously with or subsequent to its having been touched by only one [offensive] player, then all [offensive] players become and remain eligible to catch the pass (this rule was later rescinded in 1978). If the reception was illegal, the Raiders would have gained possession (by a turnover on downs), clinching a victory. After some fifteen minutes of confusion and clearing the thousands of celebrating fans off the field, it was ruled that the ball had touched both Tatum and Fuqua. After Roy Gerela's extra point, the Steelers had a remarkable 13–7 victory.

The next week, Pittsburgh lost to the Miami Dolphins in the AFC Championship game.

8. Roger Staubach. Staubach played for the Dallas Cowboys from 1969 through 1979. He was mainly a backup in his first two seasons before assuming the full-time starting duties halfway through the 1971 season. One of Staubach's early heroic efforts came in an NFC Divisional Playoff at San Francisco on December 23, 1972. He had missed most of the 1972 season with a separated shoulder, but he relieved Craig Morton during the playoff against the 49ers. In the last minute and a half, he threw touchdown passes to Billy Parks and Ron Sellers to lead Dallas to a 30–28 win.

Perhaps Staubach's most famous moment was the "Hail Mary" pass in a divisional playoff game against the Vikings at Minnesota on December 28, 1975. With seconds on the clock and the Cowboys trailing 14–10, Staubach launched a 50-yard bomb to wide receiver Drew Pearson, who caught the pass with his right hand and waltzed into the end zone for a 17–14 Dallas victory. After the game, Staubach said he threw the ball and said a "Hail Mary." Since then, any last-second pass to the end zone in a desperate attempt to score a game-winning or tying touchdown is referred to as a "Hail Mary" pass.

Staubach's last game-winning heroics came in his final regular-season game at home against the Washington Redskins on December 16, 1979. Both the Cowboys and Redskins had 10-5 records, so the game had major NFC Eastern Division and playoff implications. When Washington's John Riggins rumbled for a 66-yard touchdown run in the fourth quarter, the Cowboys were in desperation mode, trailing 34–21. Staubach, however, drove his team to a touchdown when he threw a 26-yard pass to Ron Springs to cut the Dallas deficit to 34–28. Staubach did it again, driving the Cowboys to the winning score, an 8-yard pass from himself to Tony Hill in Dallas' memorable 35–34 victory, which gave them the division title.

Two weeks later, Staubach and the Cowboys lost 21–19 at home to the Los Angeles Rams in a divisional playoff game. Staubach was a Pro Bowler in 1971 and from 1975 through 1979. He was inducted into the Pro Football Hall of Fame in 1985.

9. The Miami Dolphins. They finished 14-0 in winning the AFC Eastern Division and then defeated the Cleveland Browns and Pittsburgh Steelers in the playoffs before beating the Washington Redskins in the Super Bowl. They began the season by defeating the Chiefs 20–10 in Kansas City on September 17. Then they beat Houston, Minnesota, the New York Jets, and San Diego to improve to 5-0. Next came a nail biter in a 24–23 win over O. J. Simpson and the Buffalo Bills at home in the Orange Bowl. After that, the Dolphins crushed New England 52–0, beat the Jets 28–24, and then routed both the Cardinals and Patriots. They concluded the regular season with wins over the New York Giants and Baltimore.

Earl Morrall, who replaced Bob Griese for much of the season due to injury, was 83-of-150 for 1,360 yards with 11 touchdowns and 7 interceptions. Griese was 53-of-97 for 638 yards with 4 touchdowns and 4 picks. Larry Csonka and Mercury Morris became the first pair of running backs on the same team to each rush for 1,000 yards in the same season.

Csonka had 1,117 yards on 213 rushes with 6 touchdowns, while Morris totaled 1,000 yards on 190 carries with a dozen touchdowns. Paul Warfield had 29 receptions for 606 yards with 3 touchdowns.

In a divisional playoff at home against Cleveland, Miami trailed 14–13 halfway through the fourth quarter. Jim Kiick, however, scored from 8 yards out to put the Dolphins on top en route to a 20–14 victory. The next week, in the AFC Championship game at Pittsburgh, Miami trailed 10–7 in the third quarter before 2 short touchdown runs by Kiick had the Dolphins on top 21–10 in the fourth quarter. They held on for a 21–17 victory.

In the Super Bowl, played on January 14, 1973, at the Los Angeles Memorial Coliseum, the Dolphins took a 7–0 first-quarter lead when Griese completed a 28-yard touchdown pass to Howard Twilley. They went up 14–0 in the second quarter on a 1-yard touchdown run by Kiick. The final points of the game came by Washington in the fourth quarter

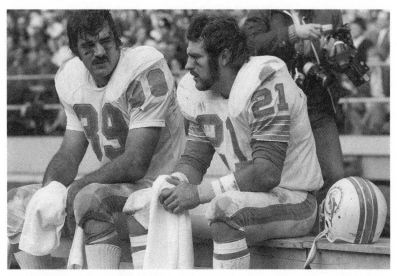

Larry Csonka and Jim Kiick taking a breather
Jerry Coli/Dreamstime.com

on a whacky play. Miami's Garo Yepremian attempted a field goal, but it was blocked. Yepremian chased the ball down, ran with it, and tried to pass it. The ball was bobbled and eventually dropped into the hands of Mike Bass, who returned it 49 yards for a touchdown. The Dolphins went on to win 14–7. They remain the only NFL team to go an entire season— regular season and postseason—undefeated and untied.

10. d. Houston Oilers. Both years, the Oilers finished in the far reaches of the AFC Central Division basement. The 1972 Oilers began the season with a 30–17 loss to Denver and a 34–13 defeat to Miami before winning their only game of the season, 26–20 over the New York Jets. Over the next five games, they scored seven or fewer points in four of them, including shutouts against Oakland and Cleveland. Houston's closest loss of the season was 18–17 to the Eagles on November 12, which dropped its record to 1-8. After that, the Oilers lost to the Packers, Chargers, Falcons, Steelers, and Bengals, respectively, the last of which came by a resounding 61–17 score.

The 1973 Oilers lost their first seven games, including a 48–20 defeat to Denver and a 42–13 loss to Cleveland. They won their lone game of the season 31–27 over Baltimore on November 4. Then they lost to the Browns again 23–13 and to Kansas City 38–14 to fall to 1-9. They scored a total of thirteen points over their next three games against New England, Oakland, and Pittsburgh. The season finale was a 27–24 defeat to Cincinnati.

11. Memorial Stadium at the University of California, Berkeley. Before 74,121 fans, Miami's eighteen-game winning streak, including the postseason, came to an end. In that game, George Blanda kicked a field goal in each quarter for a 12–0 Oakland lead. The Dolphins scored the game's final points on a 28-yard touchdown pass from Bob Griese to Jim Mandich. They won their next ten games, including a 30–26 Monday night victory over the Steelers on December 3 in which Dolphins free safety Dick Anderson intercepted 4 passes in the

first half alone, 2 of which were pick-sixes! Miami finished the season 12-2 and AFC Eastern Division champions.

The Dolphins beat the Bengals 34–16 in a divisional playoff before hosting the Raiders in a rematch in the AFC title game. In that game, Miami took a 14–0 halftime lead on two Larry Csonka touchdown runs. The teams traded field goals in the third quarter, and then the Raiders cut their deficit to 17–10 heading into the fourth quarter when Ken Stabler completed a 25-yard touchdown pass to Mike Siani. Garo Yepremian kicked a 27-yard field goal to increase the Dolphins' lead to 20–10. Csonka's 2-yard touchdown run was the icing on the cake in Miami's 27–10 win.

The Dolphins went on to defeat the Minnesota Vikings 24–7 in Super Bowl VIII.

12. Lynn Swann, Jack Lambert, John Stallworth, and Mike Webster. Swann, a wide receiver, was chosen in the first round out of the University of Southern California. Lambert, a linebacker, was selected in the second round from Kent State University. Stallworth, a wide receiver, was picked in the fourth round out of Alabama A&M University. Webster, a center, was taken in the fifth round from the University of Wisconsin. Swann, Lambert, Stallworth, and Webster joined an already stalwart roster that included Terry Bradshaw, Franco Harris, Rocky Bleier, "Mean Joe" Greene, L. C. Greenwood, Jack Ham, Mel Blount, Mike Wagner, and Andy Russell. The Pittsburgh defense came to be known as the "Steel Curtain" due to how stout and dominating it was.

The 1974 Steelers finished 10-3-1 in winning the AFC Central Division title. They beat Buffalo 32–14 in the divisional playoffs and Oakland 24–13 in the AFC Championship game. They won the franchise's first-ever championship with a 16–6 victory over the Minnesota Vikings in Super Bowl IX at Tulane Stadium in New Orleans. The 1975 Steelers finished 12-2 and won the Central Division title. They beat Baltimore 28–10 in the divisional playoffs and the Raiders 16–10 in the conference title game. They won Super Bowl X with a 21–17 triumph over the Dallas Cowboys at the Orange Bowl in Miami.

The 1976 Steelers finished 10-4 after a 1-4 start and won the Central Division again. Five of their last eight wins were by shutout, and there are those who say the 1976 edition of the Steelers was the best of the 1970s Pittsburgh teams. The Steelers beat Baltimore 40–14 in a divisional playoff, but injuries to Harris and Bleier contributed to their 24–7 loss to Oakland in the AFC Championship game. The 1977 Steelers were 9-5 and won the Central title, but they fell to the "Orange Crush" Denver Broncos 34–21 in a divisional playoff.

The 1978 Steelers finished 14-2 in winning the AFC Central title. They beat Denver 33–10 in the divisional playoffs and Houston 34–5 in the conference championship game. They outscored the Cowboys 35–31 to win Super Bowl XIII at the Orange Bowl. The 1979 Steelers were 12-4 and won the Central title again. They defeated Miami 34–14 in a divisional playoff and the Oilers again in the AFC Championship game 27–13. They won Super Bowl XIV 31–19 over the Los Angeles Rams at the Rose Bowl in Pasadena, California.

13. The Miami Dolphins and Oakland Raiders. Miami finished 11-3 and won the AFC Eastern Division title and was aiming for a third straight Super Bowl championship. Oakland was 12-2 in winning the AFC Western Division title. The game was played at the Oakland-Alameda County Coliseum. Before the game, analysts were referring to the matchup as "Super Bowl Eight and a Half" since the winner was widely expected to advance to Super Bowl IX.

The Dolphins hit pay dirt on the very first play of the game when Nat Moore silenced 52,817 rowdy Raiders fans by returning the opening kickoff 89 yards for a touchdown and a 7-0 lead. The Raiders tied the score in the second quarter when Charlie Smith caught a 31-yard touchdown pass from Ken Stabler. A 33-yard field goal by Garo Yepremian gave Miami a 10–7 halftime lead. In the third quarter, Stabler hit Fred Biletnikoff on a 13-yard touchdown pass as the Raiders forged ahead 14–10. The Dolphins took a 16–14 lead entering the fourth quarter on a 16-yard touchdown pass from Bob Griese to Paul Warfield. A 46-yard Yepremian field goal made it 19–14. Stabler gave Oakland a 21–19 lead when he connected with Cliff Branch on a spectacular 72-yard touchdown pass in which the Raiders' wide receiver fell down while catching the ball, got up, and raced into the end zone. Miami forged back ahead 26–21 when Benny Malone scored on a 23-yard run, a play in which he evaded 4 tackle attempts on the way to the end zone.

The Raiders returned the ensuing kickoff to their own 32-yard line with two minutes left. After a 6-yard completion from Stabler to Bob Moore and a short Stabler run, Stabler twice went long to Biletnikoff for gains of 18 and 20 yards. After a 4-yard pass from Stabler to Branch, Frank Pitts made a bobbling first-down catch of a Stabler pass at the Dolphins' 14-yard line. Clarence Davis then ran the ball 6 yards to the 8-yard line, where the Raiders called their final time-out. On the next play, Stabler dropped back to pass and looked for Biletnikoff in the end zone, but he was covered. With Miami's Vern Den Herder dragging him down from behind, Stabler heaved a desperation toss into a "sea of hands" in the left side of the end zone, where Davis fought his way through three Dolphins defenders to make the catch, enduring a late hit by Manny Fernandez to hold on to the ball for a touchdown. Oakland was back in the lead 28–26. The Dolphins got the ball back on the ensuing kickoff with twenty-one seconds left, but Griese was intercepted by Phil Villapiano, allowing the Raiders to run out the clock.

The next week, in the AFC Championship game, the Raiders lost at home 24–13 to the Pittsburgh Steelers.

14. Memorial Stadium in Baltimore. It happened fifteen minutes after the hometown Colts had lost 40–14 to the Pittsburgh

Steelers in an AFC Divisional Playoff game on December 19, 1976. A single-engine plane that had buzzed the stadium during the closing moments of the game crashed into the almost-empty upper-deck stands. Fortunately, most of the capacity crowd of 60,020 had left the one-sided game early. Four people were injured in the accident, the most serious being Donald Kroner, the forty-two-year-old pilot of the Maryland-registered Piper Cherokee. He was taken unconscious to a hospital with head injuries and lacerations. No one else was aboard the plane. The plane, which had come close to one of the banks of lights atop the closed end of the stadium in the waning moments of the fourth quarter, had flown in over the field from the open end. Apparently, the plane did not have enough acceleration to get over the top of the stands.

As for the game itself, the Steelers took a 6–0 first-quarter lead when Terry Bradshaw threw a 76-yard touchdown pass to Frank Lewis. Roy Gerela kicked a 45-yard field goal to make the score 9–0. Bert Jones hit Roger Carr on a 17-yard touchdown pass to pull the Colts within 9–7 after one quarter. Reggie Harrison's 1-yard touchdown run made it 16–7, and Lynn Swann's 29-yard touchdown reception from Bradshaw upped the Pittsburgh lead to 23–7. A 25-yard Gerela field goal hiked the lead to 26–7 at halftime. Swann's 11-yard touchdown catch from Bradshaw in the fourth quarter ballooned the lead to 33–7. The teams then traded meaningless touchdowns as the Steelers coasted the rest of the way.

15. The Oakland Raiders and Minnesota Vikings. The game was played on January 9, 1977, before 103,438 fans at the Rose Bowl in Pasadena, California. Both Oakland and Minnesota had had problems with winning "the big one" throughout the course of the previous nine seasons. The Raiders lost Super Bowl II to the Green Bay Packers and then lost AFL Championship games to the New York Jets in 1968 and Kansas City Chiefs in 1969. They lost AFC title

games to Baltimore in 1970, Miami in 1973, and Pittsburgh in 1974 and 1975. They were also the victims in the "Immaculate Reception" divisional playoff loss to the Steelers in 1972. The Vikings, meanwhile, were beaten soundly in Super Bowls IV, VIII, and IX against, respectively, the Chiefs, Dolphins, and Steelers.

So which team, Oakland or Minnesota, would finally win the big one? After a scoreless first quarter, the Raiders took a 3–0 second-quarter lead on a 24-yard field goal by Errol Mann. Ken Stabler threw a 1-yard touchdown pass to Dave Casper to make it 10–0. Pete Banaszak's 1-yard touchdown run upped the lead to 16–0 at halftime. In the third quarter, Mann's 40-yard field goal gave the Raiders a 19–0 lead. The Vikings finally got on the board when Fran Tarkenton hit Sammy White on an 8-yard touchdown pass to pull them within 19–7 entering the fourth quarter. Banaszak's 2-yard touchdown run gave Oakland a 26–7 lead, and Willie Brown's 75-yard interception return for a touchdown was the icing on the cake en route to a 32–14 Raiders' rout.

Stabler was 12-of-19 for 180 yards. Clarence Davis had 16 rushes for 137 yards, including a 35-yarder. Mark van Eeghen ran the ball 18 times for 73 yards. Fred Biletnikoff had 4 receptions for 79 yards, including a 48-yarder, while Casper caught 4 passes for 70 yards, including a 26-yarder.

Tarkenton was 17-of-35 for 205 yards with 2 interceptions. Chuck Foreman had 17 carries for 44 yards and 5 catches for 62 yards, including a 26-yarder. White had 5 receptions for 77 yards, while Ahmad Rashad had 3 catches for 53 yards, including a 25-yarder. Stu Voigt caught 4 for 49 yards, including a 13-yarder for a touchdown from Bob Lee.

16. c. 26. Coached by former University of Southern California legend John McKay, the Buccaneers finished 0-14 in 1976 and began the 1977 season 0-12 before winning their last two games. In their first season, they were shut out in their first two games by Houston and San Diego. They didn't score their first touchdown until Week 4 in a 42–17 loss to

Ken Stabler
Jerry Coli/Dreamstime.com

the Colts in Baltimore. Then they lost 21–0 to Cincinnati before falling 13–10 at home to the Seattle Seahawks in the battle of the expansion teams. After that, they came close in a 23–20 loss to Miami and fell 28–19 to the Chiefs and 48–13 to the Broncos to fall to 0-9. Then they got trounced 34–0 by the New York Jets and lost 24–7 to the Cleveland Browns. The Buccaneers closed their torturous season by getting blown out by Oakland (49–16), Pittsburgh (42–0), and New England (31–14). Overall, they were outscored by their opponents 412–125.

Steve Spurrier, in his final season of a ten-year career, was 156-of-311 for 1,628 yards with 7 touchdowns and 12 interceptions. Louis Carter had 171 rushes for 521 yards with a touchdown and 20 receptions for 135 yards. Morris Owens had 30 receptions for 390 yards with 6 touchdowns. John McKay, the coach's son, had 20 catches for 302 yards with a touchdown, while Bob Moore caught 23 passes for 281 yards.

The 1977 Buccaneers began the season by scoring a total of thirteen points in defeats to Philadelphia, Minnesota, Dallas, and Washington. Then they lost to Seattle 30-23 to drop to 0-5. Five of their next seven losses came by shutout. The last of them, a 10–0 loss to the Bears on December 4, dropped them to 0-12. Tampa Bay had scored a total of only fifty-three points in its first dozen games. That's an average of just 4.4 points per contest! Finally, on December 11 in New Orleans, the Bucs routed the Saints 33–14 for win number one. A week later, they beat St. Louis 17–7 for the first home win in Tampa Stadium. Although the offense got worse, the defense was much improved in 1977. Overall, the Buccaneers were outscored 223–103.

Gary Huff was 67-of-138 for 889 yards with 3 touchdowns and 13 interceptions. Randy Hedberg was 25-of-90 for 244 yards with 10 interceptions, while Jeb Blount was 37-of-89 for 522 yards with 7 picks. Number-one overall draft pick Ricky Bell ran the ball 148 times for 436 yards with a touchdown. Owens had 34 receptions for 655 yards with 3 touchdowns.

17. 12-2. Denver won the AFC Western Division by a game over the Oakland Raiders. It was the Broncos' first championship of any kind in its eighteen-year history. Their only two losses were to the Raiders and Dallas Cowboys. The Broncos beat Pittsburgh 34–21 at home at Mile High Stadium in a divisional playoff on December 24. With the game tied 14–14 in the third quarter, Riley Odoms caught a 30-yard touchdown pass from Craig Morton. In the fourth quarter, Terry Bradshaw threw a 1-yard touchdown pass to Larry Brown to tie the score 21–21. Two Jim Turner field goals gave the Broncos a 27–21 advantage, and a 34-yard touchdown pass from Morton to Jack Dolbin was the game's final points.

A week later, on New Year's Day 1978, the Broncos opposed the hated Raiders in the AFC title game at Denver. Before 74,982 raucous fans, the Raiders took a 3–0 first-quarter lead on a 20-yard field goal by Errol Mann. The Broncos took a 7–3 lead after one quarter when Morton completed a 74-yard touchdown pass to Haven Moses. In the third quarter, Denver rookie running back Rob Lytle fumbled the ball away to Oakland's Jack Tatum at the Raiders' 1-yard line, but the head linesman, Ed Marion, never saw it. Thus the Broncos retained possession of the ball. On the very next play, Jon Keyworth ran the ball into the end zone to up the Denver lead to 14–3. In the fourth quarter, Dave Casper caught a 7-yard touchdown pass from Ken Stabler to cut the Broncos' lead to 14–10. Moses caught a 12-yard touchdown pass from Morton as Denver went up 20–10. Casper caught a 17-yard touchdown pass from Stabler for the game's final points in the Broncos' 20–17 victory.

Denver's opponent in Super Bowl XII at the Louisiana Superdome on January 15 in New Orleans was Dallas. The Cowboys took a 7–0 first-quarter lead when Tony Dorsett had a 3-yard touchdown run. Two Efren Herrera field goals made it 13–0 at halftime. In the third quarter, Turner booted a 47-yard field goal to pull the Broncos within 13–3. Later in the quarter, Butch Johnson caught a diving 45-yard touchdown pass from Roger Staubach to expand the Dallas lead to 20–3. Lytle scored from a yard out to make it 20–10 after three quarters, but in the fourth quarter, Robert Newhouse completed a 29-yard touchdown pass to Golden Richards for the game's final points in the Cowboys' 27–10 victory.

18. The Minnesota Vikings and Los Angeles Rams. It was an NFC Divisional Playoff on December 26 at the Los Angeles Memorial Coliseum. The Rams had lost to the Vikings in the 1974 and 1976 NFC Championship games, and going back a little further, in the 1969 Western Conference title game. Each of those games was in cold Minnesota. This 1977 matchup was in usually sunny Southern California and figured to finally be the year that Los Angeles would defeat Minnesota in the playoffs. The Vikings were an aging team on its last legs and had to win three of its last four games just to win the weak NFC Central Division title. They barely scored more points than they yielded. The Rams, meanwhile, were loaded—on both sides of the ball. They gave up only 146 points all season long. They had also obliterated the Vikings 35–3 on a *Monday Night Football* game in late October in Los Angeles. Furthermore, Fran Tarkenton was injured in that game and hadn't played since mid-November. Bob Lee, an average quarterback at best, was his replacement. Everything pointed to a Rams' victory.

Except the weather, that is.

As luck would have it, Los Angeles was engulfed in a torrential rainstorm, and the game was played in a quagmire. Chuck Foreman led the Vikings to a 14–7 victory with 101 rushing yards on the heavy field. Minnesota head coach Bud Grant's strategy was to have Lee throw early before the field lost traction. By the end of the game, the Rams had 3 turnovers, while the Vikings had none.

The Rams took the opening kickoff and moved the ball to the Minnesota 31 yard line. However, Vikings defensive lineman Alan Page ended the drive by dropping Lawrence McCutcheon for a 1-yard loss on fourth-and-two. The Vikings took over and drove 70 yards, with Lee completing 5 of 5 passes, to a 7–0 lead on a 5-yard scoring run by Foreman. The score stayed the same until the fourth quarter. The Rams had two chances to score, but Pat Haden threw an interception to Nate Allen, and Rafael Septien missed a field goal. Minnesota's Manfred Moore returned a punt 21 yards to set up Sammy Johnson's 1-yard scoring run to increase the Vikings' lead to 14–0. With less than a minute to go, Haden threw a short touchdown pass to Harold Jackson to cut the Rams' deficit in half. The home team then recovered the ensuing onside kick, but safety Jeff Wright intercepted Haden's desperate pass in the end zone on the game's final play.

The next week, the Vikings lost 23–6 to the Dallas Cowboys in the NFC Championship game.

19. The Philadelphia Eagles. The Miracle at the Meadowlands was a fumble recovery by Eagles cornerback Herman Edwards that he returned for a touchdown at the end of a game against New York at Giants Stadium. Before the play, the playoff-hopeful Eagles trailed 17–12. The remarkable play resulted in a 19–17 victory for them. It is considered miraculous because the Giants could easily have run out the final seconds. The Eagles had no time-outs left. Everyone watching expected quarterback Joe Pisarcik to take one more snap and kneel with the ball, thus running out the clock and preserving a Giants' upset victory. Instead, he botched an attempt to hand off the ball to Larry Csonka. Edwards picked up the dropped ball and ran 26 yards for the winning score.

The Giants had opened a 2-touchdown lead in the first quarter on 2 Pisarcik touchdown passes, and did not give up the lead until the final play of the game. The Eagles, conversely, struggled, missing one of their extra-point attempts and botching the snap on the other. They found themselves down by five points, meaning they could only win the game with a touchdown as time wound down. Deep in their own territory, the Giants' Doug Kotar fumbled late in the fourth quarter, raising the Eagles' hopes of a comeback. Those were quickly put to rest, however, when rookie defensive back Odis McKinney's first NFL interception gave the Giants possession of the ball after the two-minute warning.

Fans in the stands began heading for the exits as the game seemed all but over, with no apparent remaining danger of an Eagles' comeback. Nowadays, teams in this situation let the play clock run down to the last possible second and have the quarterback take a knee. On the sidelines, disgusted Eagles head coach Dick Vermeil was turning his attention away from the field and toward the postgame press conference, where he would have to explain to reporters why his team had fallen to an inferior opponent.

Then came the Miracle at the Meadowlands.

Giants offensive coordinator Bob Gibson was fired the next morning. With angry fans already demanding that someone be held responsible for the debacle, team officials felt he had to go in hopes of saving the season. So great was the stigma of having called the play that he never worked in football at any level again. The Giants went on to finish the season with a 6-10 record. The Eagles wound up 9-7, their first winning season in twelve years, and qualified for the playoffs for the first time in eighteen years.

20. The Miami Dolphins. Campbell accumulated that total on 28 carries with 4 touchdowns, the last of which was an 81-yarder down the right sideline that put the crucial game on ice. His other 3 touchdowns came on runs of 1 yard, 6 yards, and 12 yards. He finished the season with an NFL-best 1,450 rushing yards on 302 carries with 13 touchdowns in leading the Oilers to a 10-6 record and the franchise's first playoff berth in nine years. In a 17–9 win over the same Dolphins in the AFC Wild Card Playoff game, Campbell had 26 rushes for 84 yards with a touchdown. In a 31–14

defeat of New England in a divisional playoff, he ran the ball 27 times for 118 yards with a touchdown.

The next season, in 1979, he had 368 rushes for an NFL-high 1,697 yards with a league-best 19 touchdowns in helping Houston to an 11-5 record and another playoff berth. That year, he had eleven 100-yard games, the finest of which came on Thanksgiving Day when he rushed the ball 33 times for 195 yards with 61- and 27-yard touchdowns in a 30–24 victory over the Dallas Cowboys. He led Houston to AFC title-game appearances in both 1978 and 1979.

The 5-foot-11, 232-pound Campbell was not only extremely tough for defenders to bring down, he was the linchpin behind the "Luv Ya Blue" Oilers fanaticism that was taking hold at the time. In 1980, he had 373 rushes for 1,934 yards with 13 touchdowns, all of which led the NFL. He had four 200-yard games—in wins over Tampa Bay, Cincinnati, Chicago, and Minnesota. In his final postseason game, a 27–7 loss to Oakland in the AFC Wild Card game, he had 27 rushes for 91 yards with his team's lone touchdown, a 1-yard run that gave the Oilers their only lead of the day. In 1981, he had 361 rushes for 1,376 yards with 10 touchdowns, and in 1983 he ran the ball 322 times for 1,301 yards with 12 touchdowns. He left Houston six games into the 1984 season to join the New Orleans Saints, where he finished out his career through 1985.

Overall, Campbell had 2,187 rushes for 9,407 yards with 74 touchdowns. He also had 121 receptions for 806 yards. He was a Pro Bowler from 1978 through 1981 and in 1983. He was inducted into the Pro Football Hall of Fame in 1991.

THE 1980s

AMERICA'S TOP SPECTATOR SPORT

By 1980, the NFL had overtaken Major League Baseball as the most popular sport in the country. Stricter rules on the defense in the passing game allowed quarterbacks and wide receivers to put up eye-popping numbers never before seen. Even with two players' strikes—in 1982 and 1987—the NFL had become king.

QUESTIONS

1. In the Oakland Raiders' Super Bowl–winning season of 1980, who was their starting quarterback for their first five games? *Answer on page 140.*

2. In 1981, what team accomplished the unusual feat of defeating both of that season's Super Bowl participants on the road? *Answer on page 141.*

3. The San Diego Chargers' "Air Coryell" offense was grounded in "The Freezer Bowl" by the _____. *Answer on page 142.*

4. What was the final score of "The Catch" game in which San Francisco defeated Dallas for the 1981 NFC Championship? *Answer on page 142.*

   a. 27–21
   b. 28–24
   c. 30–27
   d. 28–27

5. Why was the game between the Miami Dolphins and host New England Patriots on December 12, 1982, called the "Snowplow Game?" *Answer on page 143.*

6. What team whose offensive line was nicknamed "The Hogs" won Super Bowl XVII? *Answer on page 144.*

7. Name the six quarterbacks chosen in the first round of the renowned 1983 NFL Draft. *Answer on page 145.*

8. What backup linebacker for the Los Angeles Raiders intercepted a Joe Theismann pass and returned the ball 5 yards for a touchdown during Super Bowl XVIII? *Answer on page 147.*

9. What team's fans made famous the "Dawg Pound," beginning in 1984, which still rocks on today? *Answer on page 148.*

10. Who broke Jim Brown's all-time rushing yardage record on October 7, 1984? *Answer on page 148.*

11. I had 14 receptions for 191 yards despite a 24–20 loss to the New York Jets on October 14, 1984. Who am I? *Answer on page 150.*

12. What was the only team that beat the San Francisco 49ers in 1984? *Answer on page 151.*

13. What rookie right defensive tackle named after a kitchen appliance burst onto the national stage by lining up as a fullback and scoring a touchdown on a 1-yard run on *Monday Night Football* on October 21, 1985? *Answer on page 152.*

14. In what game on the opening weekend of the 1986 season did officials implement the new instant-replay test for the first time? *Answer on page 153.*

15. What player led the NFL with 20.5 sacks in 1986? *Answer on page 153.*

   a. Reggie White
   b. Lawrence Taylor
   c. Howie Long
   d. Mark Gastineau

16. John Elway led the Denver Broncos on a 96-yard drive in the late stages of the AFC Championship game at Cleveland on January 11, 1987, en route to a 23–20 overtime win. True or false? *Answer on page 155.*

17. How many weeks of "replacement" games were played during the 1987 NFL players' strike? *Answer on page 156.*

   a. One
   b. Two
   c. Three
   d. Four

18. What Washington running back rushed for 204 yards and 2 touchdowns in the Redskins' 42–10 rout of the Denver Broncos in Super Bowl XXII? *Answer on page 157.*

19. What two teams played in Super Bowl XXIII? *Answer on page 157.*

20. Who was San Francisco's head coach when the San Francisco 49ers won Super Bowl XXIV? *Answer on page 158.*

ANSWERS

1. Dan Pastorini. After posting a 2-2 record, Pastorini, who had been traded from the Houston Oilers before the season, broke his leg during a 31–17 home loss to the Kansas City Chiefs. Oakland fans, who had been unhappy with his performance and wanted to see backup Jim Plunkett, cheered when they realized he was hurt. Plunkett, a Heisman Trophy winner out of Stanford University and a former starter for the New England Patriots and San Francisco 49ers, had been with the Raiders as a reserve since 1978. He stepped right in and produced. He threw 2 late touchdown passes in the loss to the Chiefs. A week later, at home against San Diego in a crucial early season contest, he directed the Raiders to a 38–24 victory that included a 43-yard touchdown pass to Cliff Branch. That was the start of a six-game winning streak that lifted Oakland to 8-3. The Raiders lost a tough one, 10–7 to the Eagles, but rebounded to win three of their last four games to finish 11-5 and in the playoffs as a wild card team.

In a 27–7 home win over Houston in the AFC Wild Card game, Plunkett threw 2 touchdown passes—a 1-yarder to Todd Christensen and a 44-yarder to Arthur Whittington. In a 14–12 win over the Browns in a divisional polar playoff in frozen Cleveland, Plunkett managed to go 14-of-30 for 149 yards but with 2 interceptions, including a pick-six. The next week, the Raiders beat the Chargers 34–27 in the AFC Championship game. Plunkett was 14-of-18 for 261 yards with 2 touchdowns, the first of which was a 65-yarder to Raymond Chester on a tipped ball that gave the Raiders a 7–0 lead. Two weeks later, in Super Bowl XV at the Louisiana Superdome in New Orleans, Oakland dominated Philadelphia 27–10. Plunkett threw 3 touchdown passes, including an 80-yarder to Kenny King that gave the Raiders a 14–0 lead.

2. The Cleveland Browns. The Browns defeated the Cincinnati Bengals and San Francisco 49ers. Even more amazing is the fact that the Browns were just 5-11 that season. They beat Cincinnati 20–17 on September 20 at Riverfront Stadium. They came in 0-2, while the Bengals entered 2-0. Two Dave Jacobs field goals and a 4-yard touchdown pass from Brian Sipe to Ozzie Newsome gave Cleveland a 13–0 halftime lead. The Bengals cut it to 13–10 on a Jim Breech 21-yard field goal in the third quarter and a 41-yard touchdown pass from Ken Anderson to Cris Collinsworth in the fourth quarter. The Browns expanded their lead to 20–10 on a 12-yard touchdown run by Mike Pruitt. Pete Johnson's 1-yard touchdown run accounted for the game's final points.

On November 15 at Candlestick Park, the Browns beat San Francisco 15–12. The Browns were 4-6 entering the game, while the 49ers, on their way to victory in Super Bowl XVI, were 8-2. Four Ray Wersching field goals and one by Matt Bahr plus a Cleveland safety added up to a 12–5 'Niners lead after three quarters. The game's only touchdown was when Sipe threw a 21-yard touchdown pass to Reggie Rucker, which tied the score. Bahr booted a 24-yard field goal that won the game.

3. Cincinnati Bengals. The Bengals beat the Chargers 27–7 in the AFC Championship game on January 10, 1982, at frozen Riverfront Stadium in Cincinnati. The game was played in the coldest temperature in NFL history in terms of wind chill, minus fifty-nine degrees. Despite the Bengals' dominating 40–17 win over the Chargers in Southern California

during the regular season, the two teams' meeting in the conference title game was expected to be a very competitive contest.

The Chargers' offense featured quarterback Dan Fouts, receivers Charlie Joiner and Wes Chandler, and tight end Kellen Winslow. San Diego also had two superb running backs, Chuck Muncie, who led the NFL with 19 touchdowns (all rushing), and multitalented rookie James Brooks, who finished the season with 2,093 all-purpose yards. The Chargers had scored an NFL-high 478 points during the regular season. The Bengals weren't chopped liver, however. They had league Most Valuable Player Ken Anderson at quarterback, rookie wide receiver Cris Collinsworth, tight end Dan Ross, running back Pete Johnson, and offensive left tackle Anthony Munoz.

The Bengals took a 3–0 first-quarter lead on a 31-yard field goal by Jim Breech. They increased their lead to 10–0 after one quarter on an 8-yard touchdown pass from Anderson to M. L. Harris. The Chargers cut their deficit to 10–7 when Fouts connected with Winslow on a 33-yard touchdown pass. Johnson's 1-yard touchdown run upped the Cincinnati lead to 17–7 at the half. Breech kicked a 38-yard field goal to make it 20–7 entering the fourth quarter. Anderson hit Don Bass on a 3-yard touchdown pass for the game's final points.

The Bengals went on to lose to San Francisco 26–21 in Super Bowl XVI.

4. d. 28–27. The game was played on January 10, 1982, at Candlestick Park in San Francisco. With fifty-eight seconds left and the 49ers facing third-and-three at the Dallas 6 yard line, San Francisco wide receiver Dwight Clark made a leaping grab from Joe Montana in the back of the end zone, enabling the 49ers to defeat the Cowboys 28–27. The Catch was the crowning glory of a fourteen-play, 83-yard drive engineered by Montana. The game represented the end of the Cowboys' domination in the NFC since the conference's inception in

1970 and the beginning of the 49ers' rise as an NFL dynasty in the 1980s.

The 49ers took a 7–0 first-quarter lead when Freddie Solomon caught an 8-yard touchdown pass from Montana. Rafael Septien kicked a 44-yard field goal to make it 7–3. Danny White threw a 26-yard touchdown pass to Tony Hill to put the Cowboys on top 10–7 after one quarter. In the second quarter, Montana hit Clark on a 20-yard scoring strike as the home team forged ahead 14–10. Tony Dorsett's 5-yard touchdown run put the Cowboys back on top 17–14 at halftime. The 'Niners retook the lead 21–17 after three quarters on a short touchdown run by Johnny Davis. In the fourth quarter, Septien's 22-yard field goal pulled the Cowboys within 21–20. They forged ahead 27–21 on a 21-yard touchdown pass from White to Doug Cosbie. Then came the 49ers' memorable drive to The Catch.

5. Schaefer Stadium's snowplow operator, Mark Henderson, cleared a spot on the snowy field specifically for New England kicker John Smith so he could boot a field goal to give the Patriots a 3–0 lead en route to a win by the same score. The night before the game, heavy rains had soaked the AstroTurf surface at the stadium. The field froze over, and conditions were made significantly worse as a snowstorm hit during the game. As a result, an emergency ground rule was put into play where the officials could call time-out and allow the ground crew to use a snowplow to clear the yard markers. Despite this rule, the ground crew could not plow often enough to keep the field clear.

The two teams remained scoreless late into the fourth quarter. With four minutes and forty-five seconds left and on-field conditions worsening, Patriots head coach Ron Meyer ordered Henderson, a convicted burglar on a work-release program from MCI-Norfolk at the time, to clear a spot on the field specifically for Smith. At first, no one had thought it suspicious, assuming that the plow would go straight across and allow for a more accurate measurement (which turned out to be 33 yards). Instead, the plow veered left, directly in front of the goal post, giving Smith a clean spot from which to kick. Matt Cavanaugh held for the boot, which was successful.

Dolphins head coach Don Shula, angry with the move and believing it was against NFL rules, pointed out that the league's unfair act clause allowed the league to overturn the game result. He met with NFL commissioner Pete Rozelle several days later, and although Rozelle agreed with Shula that the use of the plow gave the Patriots an unfair advantage, he said that he had never reversed the result of a game and was not going to start doing so for any reason.

6. The Washington Redskins. Although the nickname originated during training camp in 1982, The Hogs lasted through the early 1990s. The original Hogs were comprised of center Jeff Bostic, left guard Russ Grimm, right guard Mark May, left tackle Joe Jacoby, right tackle George Starke, guard Fred Dean, and tight ends Don Warren and Rick Walker. The original Hogs provided protection for running back John Riggins and quarterback Joe Theismann. The 1982 Redskins finished with a record of 8-1 and in first place in the NFC in a strike-shortened season. They beat Philadelphia and Tampa Bay before the strike occurred. When the strike ended, the 'Skins stayed hot. They beat the Giants and Eagles before losing 24–10 to Dallas. They concluded the regular season by beating the Cardinals twice, the Giants, and the Saints. They defeated Detroit 31-7 in the first round of the expanded postseason. The next week, they beat the Vikings 21-7, and after that, they knocked off the Cowboys 31–17 in the NFC Championship game.

In the Super Bowl, which was played on January 30, 1983, at the Rose Bowl in Pasadena, California, the Redskins defeated the Miami Dolphins 27–17. The Dolphins took a 7–0 lead after the first quarter when David Woodley threw a 76-yard touchdown pass to Jimmy Cefalo. After the teams traded field goals in the second quarter, Theismann hit Alvin Garrett on a short touchdown pass to tie the score at 10.

Fulton Walker returned the ensuing kickoff 98 yards for a touchdown to put Miami back in the lead 17–10 at halftime. The score was 17–13 in the fourth quarter when Riggins rumbled for a 43-yard touchdown run and a 20–17 Washington lead. The Redskins scored the game's final points on a 6-yard touchdown pass from Theismann to Charlie Brown.

7. John Elway, Todd Blackledge, Jim Kelly, Tony Eason, Ken O'Brien, and Dan Marino. Elway was the first overall pick by the Baltimore Colts out of Stanford University. When Elway refused to play for the pitiful Colts and threatened to return to the New York Yankees organization in which he had played for a short time during the summer of 1982, Baltimore still drafted him, but eventually the Colts traded him to the Denver Broncos. After a somewhat rough rookie season in 1983, Elway soon turned into one of the finest quarterbacks in the NFL, notable for his velocity, running ability, and penchant for leading late-game comebacks. He led the Broncos to five Super Bowls, the last two of which they won in 1997 and 1998, his final season.

Blackledge was the seventh overall choice by the Kansas City Chiefs from Penn State University. He played for the Chiefs from 1983 through 1987 and the Pittsburgh Steelers in 1988 and 1989. He was a sporadic starter throughout his career. In 1986, he helped Kansas City earn its first playoff berth in fifteen years.

Kelly was the fourteenth overall selection by the Buffalo Bills from the University of Miami. He spent 1984 and 1985 with the Houston Gamblers of the United States Football League before joining the Bills in 1986. It didn't take long for him to help turn the Bills into a regular playoff contender. In fact, he led them to four straight Super Bowls from 1990 through 1993. He played with the Bills through 1996.

Eason was the fifteenth overall pick by the New England Patriots out of the University of Illinois. He played for the Patriots from 1983 through 1989. During the 1989 season, he left the Pats and concluded his career with the New York

Dan Marino prepares to pass.
Jerry Coli/Dreamstime.com

Jets through 1990. Although he was a backup for most of his career, he helped New England to postseason berths in 1985 and 1986. He threw 6 passes, completing one of them, and was sacked three times in the Patriots' 46–10 loss to the Chicago Bears in Super Bowl XX.

O'Brien was the twenty-fourth overall choice by the New York Jets out of the University of California-Davis. He played for the Jets from 1984 through 1992 and for the Philadelphia Eagles in 1993. He was a starter for most of his career, with his finest seasons coming in 1985 and 1986 when he led the Jets to the playoffs.

Marino was the twenty-seventh overall selection by the Miami Dolphins from the University of Pittsburgh. He played for the Dolphins from 1983 through 1999. He had one of the quickest releases ever. In 1984, he passed for an NFL-best 5,084 yards and 48 touchdowns in leading Miami to Super Bowl XIX. He never made it back to the "big game," but he had one of the greatest careers by a quarterback. He threw for more than 4,000 yards five more times and passed for 30 or more touchdowns three other times.

8. Jack Squirek. Squirek was a second-round draft choice of the Raiders in 1982 out of the University of Illinois. He played for them from 1982 through 1985 and for the Miami Dolphins in 1986. He had only one other interception in his career. A few moments before Squirek's pick-six late in the second quarter of Super Bowl XVIII, a Raiders' drive stalled when Jim Plunkett's third-down pass was incomplete, but Ray Guy's 27-yard punt pinned Washington at their own 12-yard line with 12 seconds left in the first half. On the Redskins' first play came Squirek's memorable interception. It was the dagger to the Redskins' heart as it expanded the Los Angeles lead to 21–3 at halftime. With the score 21–9 in the third quarter, Marcus Allen scored on a 5-yard run to make it 28–9. Later in the quarter, Allen, the game's Most Valuable Player, put the icing on the cake with a 74-yard

touchdown run that upped the Raiders' lead to 35–9. The final score was 38–9.

9. The Cleveland Browns. The Browns were having a terrible season, so there wasn't much for fans to cheer. During a home game at Cleveland Stadium, Hanford Dixon and Frank Minnifield began barking to fans in the bleachers section. Little did the Browns' starting cornerbacks know that their woofing would be the start of something big. Thousands of fans in the bleachers section began barking their lungs out, dressed in dog masks with their faces painted brown, orange, and white. Some even ate dog biscuits! The bleachers section had become a "Dawg Pound," which is what it came to be known as, not only in Cleveland but nationally. The team soon began winning, which increased the barking even more. Even during the mostly less-than-stellar seasons in the early 1990s, the Dawg Pound continued its crazy canine antics.

When the expansion Browns of 1999 arrived three years after the original Browns relocated to Baltimore, the Dawg Pound was reborn as the official name of the Cleveland Browns Stadium (now FirstEnergy Stadium) bleachers section. The new Pound differs from the original one in having two decks. The present Dawg Pound certainly lacks the charm and madness of the original Dawg Pound in which fans would hurl biscuits, batteries, eggs, and other objects at opposing players. Their rowdiness made life so miserable for opposing teams that, at one point during a victory over the Denver Broncos in 1989, officials were forced to move play to the closed end of the stadium. But, all in all, the positives outweighed the negatives.

10. Walter Payton. "Sweetness" broke Brown's record of 12,312 yards during a 20–7 win over the New Orleans Saints at Soldier Field in Chicago. In that game, Payton had 32 rushes for 154 yards, including a 25-yarder, with a 1-yard touchdown. In that 1984 season, he had 381 carries for 1,684 yards with 11 touchdowns and 45 receptions for

Walter Payton
Jerry Coli/Dreamstime.com

368 yards in leading the Bears to a 10-6 record and the NFC Central Division title. In a 23–19 upset of Washington in a divisional playoff, Chicago's first postseason win in twenty-one years, he ran the ball 24 times for 104 yards. Despite Chicago's losing 23–0 to San Francisco in the conference championship game, he managed 22 rushes for 92 yards, including a 20-yarder. The next season, in 1985, he rushed the ball 324 times for 1,551 yards with 9 touchdowns and had 49 catches for 483 yards with 2 touchdowns. In a 21–0 divisional playoff win over the Giants, he ran the ball 27 times for 93 yards. In the Bears' 46–10 win over New England in Super Bowl XX, he had 22 carries for 61 yards.

Payton began his career in 1975 with the Bears. His finest season was in 1977 when he had 339 rushes for 1,852 yards with 14 touchdowns, all of which led the NFL. He also had 27 receptions for 269 yards with 2 touchdowns. In the process, he led the Bears to their first postseason appearance since 1963. He had two 200-yard rushing games that year—205 in a win over Green Bay on October 30 and 275 in a win over Minnesota on November 20. The latter was an NFL record for twenty-three years until Cincinnati's Corey Dillon broke it in 2000. Payton's yearly rushing totals continued to impress—1,395 in 1978, 1,610 in 1979, 1,460 in 1980, and 1,222 in 1981. Despite a 1979 wild card playoff loss to Philadelphia, he managed 16 rushes for 67 yards with 2 touchdowns and 3 receptions for 52 yards, including a 31-yarder.

Payton played for the Bears through 1987. Overall, he had 3,838 rushes for 16,726 yards with 110 touchdowns and had 492 receptions for 4,538 yards with 15 touchdowns. He was a Pro Bowler from 1976 through 1980 and from 1983 through 1986. He was enshrined into the Pro Football Hall of Fame in 1993.

11. Ozzie Newsome. The game was played at Cleveland Stadium. I had a 52-yard reception from Paul McDonald that day. I played tight end for the Browns from 1978 through

1990. I was a first-round draft pick of theirs from the University of Alabama in 1978. I got off to a fine start as I scored on a 33-yard end-around in my very first game, a victory over the San Francisco 49ers in Week 1 of my rookie season. That year, I had 38 receptions for 589 yards with 2 touchdowns. In 1979, I had 55 receptions for 781 yards with 9 touchdowns, and in 1980 I had 51 catches for 594 yards with 3 touchdowns. I led the Browns in receptions and receiving yards every season from 1981 through 1985 and in touchdown receptions in 1979, 1981, and from 1983 through 1985. My 1,002 yards receiving in 1981 were the most by a Browns player in thirteen years.

In the strike-shortened season of 1982, I had 49 receptions for 633 yards with 3 touchdowns. I amassed a team-record 89 catches (tied by Kellen Winslow Jr., in 2006) in both 1983 and 1984 for 970 and 1,001 yards, respectively. I caught 62 passes for 711 yards with 5 touchdowns in 1985. That season, in a 24–21 loss to Miami in an AFC Divisional Playoff, I caught a 16-yard touchdown pass from Bernie Kosar. I had 6 receptions for 114 yards in a 23–20 double-overtime win against the Jets in a divisional playoff on January 3, 1987. In a 38–21 divisional playoff win over Indianapolis on January 9, 1988, I caught 4 passes for 65 yards.

Overall, I had 662 receptions for 7,980 yards with 47 touchdowns. I was a Pro Bowler in 1981, 1984, and 1985 and was inducted into the Pro Football Hall of Fame in 1999.

12. The Pittsburgh Steelers. After starting the season 6-0, the 49ers hosted the 3-3 Steelers on October 14 at Candlestick Park. The Steelers took a 7–0 lead after one quarter when Rich Erenberg scored on a 2-yard run. In the second quarter, Gary Anderson kicked a 48-yard field goal to give them a 10–0 lead. Joe Montana's 7-yard touchdown run pulled the 49ers within 10–7 at halftime. Ray Wersching's 30-yard field goal in the fourth quarter tied the score at 10. Wendell

Tyler's 7-yard touchdown run put San Francisco ahead 17–10. John Stallworth caught a 6-yard touchdown pass from Mark Malone to tie the score. Anderson kicked a 21-yard field goal to give Pittsburgh a 20–17 victory.

The loss to the Steelers was just a bump in the road as the 49ers rolled through the rest of their schedule, winning their last nine games to finish 15-1 and NFC Western Division champions. They beat the New York Giants 21–10 in a divisional playoff and then easily defeated the Chicago Bears 23–0 in the NFC title game.

The 49ers played the Miami Dolphins in Super Bowl XIX on January 20, 1985, at Stanford Stadium in Stanford, California. With the Dolphins up 3–0 in the first quarter, Montana threw a 33-yard touchdown pass to Carl Monroe for a 7–3 San Francisco lead. Dan Marino hit Dan Johnson on a short touchdown pass to give Miami a 10–7 lead after one quarter. The 49ers scored three straight touchdowns in the second quarter, the last of which came on a 6-yard run by Montana, to put the 'Niners on top 28–10. Two Uwe von Schamann field goals brought the Dolphins within 28–16 at the half. In the third quarter, Wersching booted a 27-yard field goal for a 31–16 San Francisco lead. The 49ers put the icing on the cake later in the third when Montana hit Roger Craig on a 16-yard touchdown pass for the final points of the game. The 49ers cruised the rest of the way to a 38–16 triumph.

13. William "The Refrigerator" Perry. Perry's nickname was due to his enormous size—6 feet, 2 inches and 335 pounds. The touchdown he scored that night was for the Chicago Bears, for whom he played through 1993. He spent part of 1993 and 1994 with Philadelphia. His touchdown on *Monday Night Football* came during a 23–7 win over the Green Bay Packers at Soldier Field in Chicago. Bears head coach Mike Ditka had decided to use Perry as a fullback when the team was near the opponent's goal line or in fourth-and-short situations, either as a ball carrier or a lead blocker for

star Walter Payton. Ditka stated the inspiration for using Perry as a fullback came to him during 5-yard sprint exercises. During his rookie season, Perry rushed for one other touchdown in a win over Atlanta and caught a touchdown pass in Chicago's second meeting with Green Bay.

Perry even had the opportunity to run the ball during Super Bowl XX that season as a nod to his popularity and contributions to the team's success. The first time he got the ball, he was tackled for a 1-yard loss while attempting to throw his first NFL pass on a halfback option play. The second time he got the ball, he scored a touchdown, running over Patriots linebacker Larry McGrew in the process, for the Bears' final touchdown in a 46–10 romp over the New England Patriots.

14. The game between the Cleveland Browns and Chicago Bears on September 7 at Soldier Field in Chicago. It came on the fourth play of the game and confirmed a touchdown for the Browns. On the play, a check of a replay confirmed that Cleveland safety Al Gross had recovered a fumbled Bears' snap before sliding out of the end zone, giving the Browns a 7–0 lead. The Bears came back and went on to win the game 41–31. In March 1986, the NFL had adopted the use of instant replay to aid officials on plays involving possession and inbound calls. Two calls had been changed by the instant replay during the 1986 preseason.

15. b. Lawrence Taylor. Taylor achieved the feat as a right outside linebacker for the New York Giants team that finished 14-2 in winning the NFC Eastern Division and rolled through the playoffs on their way to the Super Bowl XXI championship. "L.T." was dominant during that 1986 season. He had 4 sacks in one game, a 35–3 rout of Philadelphia on October 12. He totaled 3 sacks in a game three times—in wins over Washington on October 27, the Eagles on November 9, and Washington again on December 7. He returned an interception 34

Lawrence Taylor
Jerry Coli/Dreamstime.com

yards for a touchdown in a 49–3 demolition of San Francisco in the divisional playoffs.

Taylor began his career in 1981 with the Giants. He amassed 11.5 sacks in 1984, 13 sacks in 1985, 12 sacks in 1987, 15.5 sacks in 1988, 15 sacks in 1989, and 10.5 sacks in 1990. He played with the Giants through 1993.

Overall, Taylor totaled 134 sacks. He had 8.5 postseason sacks. He is considered to be one of the greatest players in the history of professional football. He has been ranked as the greatest defensive player in NFL annals by former players, coaches, media members, and news outlets such as the NFL Network and the *Sporting News*. He was a disruptive force and is credited with changing the pass rushing schemes, offensive line play, and offensive formations used in the NFL. He was a Pro Bowler from 1981 through 1990. He was inducted into the Pro Football Hall of Fame in 1999.

16. False. He led Denver on a 98-yard drive to tie the score 20–20 with 37seconds left. It quickly became known as "The Drive." The Broncos finished 11-5 in 1986, won the AFC Western Division title, and then beat New England in the divisional playoffs. The Browns were 12-4, won the AFC Central Division title, and then defeated the Jets in a memorable double-overtime comeback win in a divisional playoff.

In the Denver–Cleveland game, the Browns took a 7–0 lead after one quarter when Bernie Kosar hit Herman Fontenot on a 6-yard touchdown pass. The Broncos cut their deficit to 7–3 in the second quarter on a 19-yard Rich Karlis field goal and then forged ahead 10–7 on a Gerald Willhite 1-yard touchdown run. Mark Moseley's 29-yard field goal tied the score 10–10 at halftime. The teams traded field goals in the third quarter. What seemed to be the play of the game occurred when Kosar completed a 48-yard catch-and-run to Brian Brennan with five minutes and forty-three seconds to go in the game, giving the Browns a 20–13 lead. After Gene Lang muffed the ensuing kickoff, pinning the Broncos on their own 2-yard line, Elway directed The Drive to the tying touchdown. Karlis's 33-yard field goal in sudden death was the game winner. In Super Bowl XXI, Denver lost 39–20 to the New York Giants.

17. c. Three. The third week of games was cancelled, and then weeks four through six were played with mostly replacement players. Approximately 15 percent of the regular players chose to cross picket lines to play during the strike. Prominent players who did so included New York Jets defensive end Mark Gastineau, Dallas Cowboys defensive tackle Randy White, San Francisco 49ers quarterback Joe Montana, Cleveland Browns tight end Ozzie Newsome, and Seattle Seahawks wide receiver Steve Largent. The replacement players were mostly those left out of work by the recent folding of the Canadian Football League's Montreal Alouettes and the 1986 dissolution of the United States Football League, as well as others who had been preseason cuts, had long left professional football, and other assorted oddities (such as cinematographer Todd Schlopy, who, despite having never played professional football before or after the strike, served as placekicker for his hometown Buffalo Bills for the three games during the strike).

The replacement players, called to play on short notice and having little chance to gel as teammates, were widely treated with scorn by the press and general public, including name-calling, public shaming, and accusations of being scabs. The games played by these replacement players were regarded with even less legitimacy—attendance plummeted to fewer than 10,000 fans at many of the games in smaller markets and cities with strong union presence, with a low of 4,074 for the lone replacement game played in Philadelphia—but nonetheless were counted as regular NFL games. Final television revenues were down by about 20 percent, a smaller drop than the networks had expected.

The defending Super Bowl champion New York Giants went 0-3 in the replacement games, ultimately costing them a chance to qualify for the playoffs and defend their 1986 NFL championship. The final replacement game was a *Monday Night Football* matchup on October 19, the Redskins at the Cowboys. Along with the Eagles, the Redskins were the only other NFL team not to have any players cross the picket line but were surprising 13–7 victors over the Cowboys, who had plenty of big-name players cross the picket line.

18. Timmy Smith. The rookie from Texas Tech University had rushed for only 126 yards during the regular season. In playoff wins over Chicago and Minnesota, he showed flashes by rushing for 66 yards and 72 yards, respectively. But it was in the Super Bowl where he stunned the Broncos—and the nation—with his magnificent performance on January 31, 1988, at Jack Murphy Stadium in San Diego. His yardage total came on 22 carries, including 58- and 4-yard touchdown runs. He also caught 1 pass for 9 yards. Incredibly, he would play just two more seasons, 1988 with the Redskins and one game with Dallas in 1990.

Amazingly, Smith was not the Most Valuable Player of Super Bowl XXII. Doug Williams was. The former Tampa Bay quarterback did most of his damage in the second quarter, when the Redskins scored 35 points. In that remarkable quarter, Williams threw 4 touchdown passes—80- and 50-yarders to Ricky Sanders, a 27-yarder to Gary Clark, and an 8-yarder to Clint Didier. Williams was 18-of-29 for 340 yards with an interception. Sanders had 9 catches for 193 yards.

19. The Cincinnati Bengals and San Francisco 49ers. The Bengals finished 12-4, won the AFC Central Division title, and defeated Seattle and Buffalo in the playoffs. The 49ers were 10-6, won the NFC Western Division title, and beat Minnesota and Chicago in the playoffs.

The Super Bowl was played on January 22, 1989, at Joe Robbie Stadium in Miami. With the scored tied 6–6 on 4 field goals, the Bengals took a 7-point lead in the third quarter when Stanford Jennings returned a kickoff 93 yards for a touchdown. The 49ers tied the score 13–13 in the fourth quarter on a 14-yard touchdown pass from Joe Montana to Jerry Rice. The Bengals took a 16–13 lead when Jim Breech kicked a 40-yard field goal with three minutes and twenty seconds left. Montana responded by leading the 'Niners on an 11-play, 92-yard drive that was capped by a 10-yard touchdown pass he threw to John Taylor with thirty-nine seconds remaining. San Francisco's defense sealed the 20–16 victory when Boomer Esiason's pass to Cris Collinsworth was broken up as time expired.

Montana was 23-of-36 for 357 yards. Roger Craig had 17 rushes for 71 yards and 8 receptions for 101 yards, including a 40-yarder. Rice had 11 catches for 215 yards, including a 44-yarder. Esiason was 11-of-25 for 144 yards with an interception. Ickey Woods ran the ball 20 times for 79 yards. Collinsworth had 3 receptions for 40 yards, James Brooks had 2 catches for 32 yards, and Eddie Brown caught 3 passes for 32 yards.

20. George Seifert. Seifert took over following Bill Walsh's retirement after leading the 49ers to the Super Bowl XXIII title the previous season. Seifert had been the team's defensive coordinator from 1983 through 1988. Of all the great 49ers teams in the 1980s and 1990s, Seifert's 1989 squad just may have been the best. The season began with wins over Indianapolis, Tampa Bay, and Philadelphia. Then came a 13–12 loss at home to the Los Angeles Rams. After that, the 49ers won six straight games, the last of which was a 45–3 rout of the Falcons, to improve to 9-1. After a 21–17 home loss to Green Bay, they won their last five games, including a revenge-minded 30–27 victory over the Rams in Los Angeles to finish 14-2 and NFC Western Division champions.

Overall, Montana was 271-of-386 for 3,521 yards with 26 touchdowns and 8 interceptions. Roger Craig rushed the ball 271 times for 1,054 yards with 6 touchdowns and had

Joe Montana
Jerry Coli/Dreamstime.com

49 receptions for 473 yards with a touchdown. Jerry Rice had 82 catches for both a league-leading 1,483 yards and 17 touchdowns, while John Taylor caught 60 passes for 1,077 yards with 10 touchdowns. Brent Jones had 40 receptions for 500 yards with 4 touchdowns.

The 49ers destroyed the Vikings and Rams in the playoffs en route to a Super Bowl matchup with the Denver Broncos. The game was played on January 28, 1990, at the Louisiana Superdome in New Orleans. It was all San Francisco from the start. The 49ers took a 7–0 first-quarter lead when Rice caught a 20-yard touchdown pass from Montana. After a 42-yard field goal by David Treadwell made the score 7–3, Jones caught a 7-yard touchdown pass from Montana for a 13–3 San Francisco lead after one quarter. In the second quarter, Tom Rathman had a 1-yard touchdown run, and then Montana threw a 38-yard touchdown pass to Rice as the 49ers took a 27–3 halftime lead. Two more scoring strikes from Montana to Rice and Taylor had the 'Niners up 41–10 after three quarters. Rathman and Craig scored on short runs to make the final score 55–10.

THE 1990s

PRO FOOTBALL'S AERIAL SHOW

The 1990s brought even more astronomical numbers in the passing game. Holdovers from the previous decade like Dan Marino, John Elway, Jim Everett, and Warren Moon continued their assault on the record books, while newcomers such as Brett Favre and Drew Bledsoe began their onslaught through the air.

QUESTIONS

1. What linebacker with the initials D.T. had 7 sacks in one game on November 11, 1990? *Answer on page 165.*

2. What AFC quarterback passed for 527 yards in a 27–10 victory over Kansas City on December 16, 1990? *Answer on page 165.*

3. How long was the field-goal attempt that Buffalo's Scott Norwood missed with just seconds remaining in the Bills' 20–19 loss to the New York Giants in Super Bowl XXV? *Answer on page 166.*

a. 43 yards

b. 45 yards

c. 47 yards

d. 49 yards

4. What team drafted Brett Favre? *Answer on page 167.*

5. What quarterback led the Washington Redskins to the Super Bowl XXVI championship? *Answer on page 168.*

6. The two teams that played in Super Bowl XXVII and Super Bowl XXVIII were the _____ and _____. *Answer on page 169.*

7. What Dallas Cowboy made a failed attempt at a recovery of a blocked field goal that cost the Cowboys a victory against the Miami Dolphins on Thanksgiving Day 1993? *Answer on page 170.*

8. What player with the initials T.T. has the distinction of having scored the NFL's first-ever two-point conversion? *Answer on page 170.*

9. After spending thirteen seasons and enjoying much success with San Francisco, Joe Montana was in his second season with Kansas City in 1994. After leading the Chiefs to the playoffs the year before, he was trying to do it again. He and the Chiefs were 3-2 heading into a Monday night game at Mile High Stadium in Denver on October 17. The game turned out to be quite a duel between Montana and John Elway. Who won? *Answer on page 171.*

10. What current NFL head coach came to the rescue, going from third-string quarterback to hero, on Thanksgiving Day 1994? *Answer on page 172.*

11. What AFC West team opposed the San Francisco 49ers in Super Bowl XXIX? *Answer on page 173.*

12. What two teams who played one another in two Super Bowls during the 1970s opposed each other in Super Bowl XXX? *Answer on page 173.*

13. The Jacksonville Jaguars and Carolina Panthers were expansion teams in 1995. By 1996, the two teams advanced all the way to their respective conference championship games, the Jaguars in the AFC and the Panthers in the NFC. To what teams did each of them lose in the conference title games? *Answer on page 174.*

14. In each of John Elway's first three Super Bowls in the late 1980s, he and the Denver Broncos were destroyed. It was a different story, however, in his final two seasons, 1997 and 1998. What two teams did he and the Broncos defeat in Super Bowl XXXII and Super Bowl XXXIII? *Answer on page 175.*

15. What three seasons was the city of Cleveland without the Browns after they relocated to Baltimore? *Answer on page 176.*

    a. 1994, 1995, 1996
    b. 1995, 1996, 1997
    c. 1996, 1997, 1998
    d. 1997, 1998, 1999

16. The expansion Cleveland Browns selected the University of Kentucky's _____ with the number-one overall pick in the 1999 NFL Draft. *Answer on page 176.*

17. Match the players on the left with their nicknames on the right. *Answer on page 177.*

Brett Favre	"Woody"
Randall Cunningham	"Magic"
Richard Dent	"The Minister of Defense"
Neal Anderson	"Thunder"
Andre Rison	"Prime Time"
Reggie White	"Sackman"
Deion Sanders	"Bad Moon"
Rod Woodson	"Gunslinger"
Ricky Watters	"Charley"
Desmond Howard	"The Ultimate Weapon"

18. What Cleveland Browns offensive tackle was hit in the eye with a penalty flag on December 19, 1999? *Answer on page 178.*

19. What team did the Tennessee Titans defeat in the "Music City Miracle" game on January 8, 2000? *Answer on page 178.*

20. The St. Louis Rams defeated the _____ in Super Bowl XXXIV. *Answer on page 180.*

   a. Tennessee Titans
   b. New England Patriots
   c. Pittsburgh Steelers
   d. Denver Broncos

ANSWERS

1. Derrick Thomas. The Kansas City Chiefs' right outside line-backer sacked the Seattle Seahawks' Dave Krieg seven times despite a 17–16 defeat at Arrowhead Stadium in Kansas City. Krieg was sacked two other times that day, by Neil Smith and Chris Martin. Thomas broke the NFL record of 6 sacks in one game, set by San Francisco's Fred Dean on November 13, 1983, against New Orleans. Thomas almost got sack number eight, but, as time expired, Krieg wriggled free of Thomas and heaved a desperation 25-yard touchdown pass to Paul Skansi in the end zone. Skansi, surrounded by de-fenders, leaped high in the middle of the end zone to make the catch. Norm Johnson booted the extra point to give the Seahawks the victory over the stunned Chiefs.

   Thomas led the NFL in 1990 with 20 sacks. He recorded 6 sacks in a game against the Oakland Raiders on September 6, 1998. He played with Kansas City from 1989 through 1999 and, overall, totaled 126.5 sacks. He was picked for the Pro Bowl from 1989 through 1997 and was inducted into the Pro Football Hall of Fame in 2009.

2. Warren Moon. Moon accomplished the feat as a member of the Houston Oilers and did it at Arrowhead Stadium in Kansas City. Moon's yardage total is tied for second all-time with Matt Schaub, who did it as a member of the Houston Texans on November 18, 2012, against the Jacksonville Jag-uars. The all-time record is held by Norm Van Brocklin, who, as a member of the Los Angeles Rams, threw for 554 yards against the New York Yanks on September 28, 1951.

   In the Oilers–Chiefs game, Moon passed for 3 touchdowns, including the one that gave Houston a 7–0 first-quarter lead, a 24-yarder to Tony Jones. Moon's second touchdown pass was an 87-yarder to Haywood Jeffires in the third quarter, which upped the Oilers' lead to 17–7. Moon's last touchdown pass was a 2-yarder to Jones in the fourth quarter for the game's final points. In that 1990 season, Moon was

362-of-584 for 4,689 yards with 33 touchdowns, all of which led the NFL. He also threw 13 interceptions.

Moon played for the Oilers from 1984 through 1993, the Minnesota Vikings from 1994 through 1996, the Seattle Seahawks in 1997 and 1998, and the Chiefs in 1999 and 2000. In 1991, he was 404-of-655 for 4,690 yards, all league highs. He also threw 23 touchdown passes but a league-high 21 interceptions. With the Vikings, he eclipsed 4,000 yards, passing twice, in his first two seasons. He led the Oilers to the playoffs from 1987 through 1993 and directed the Vikings to the playoffs in 1994.

Overall, Moon completed 3,988 of 6,823 passes for 49,325 yards with 291 touchdowns and 233 interceptions. He was a Pro Bowler from 1988 through 1995 and in 1997. He was enshrined into the Pro Football Hall of Fame in 2006.

3. c. 47 yards. Norwood's kick sailed wide right, less than a yard outside of the upright. To this day, it is the only potential Super Bowl–winning field-goal try in which the kicker's team would have lost had the kick missed. After Norwood's miss, the Giants ran out the clock. The game was played on January 27, 1991, at Tampa Stadium in Tampa, Florida. The Giants took a 3–0 first-quarter lead on a 28-yard field goal by Matt Bahr. Norwood's 23-yard field goal tied the score after one quarter. In the second quarter, the Bills took a 10–3 lead on a 1-yard touchdown run by Don Smith. They upped their lead to 12–3 when Bruce Smith tackled Jeff Hostetler in the Giants' end zone for a safety. Later in the quarter, Hostetler threw a 14-yard touchdown pass to Stephen Baker to cut the Giants' deficit to 12–10 at halftime. Ottis Anderson scored on a short run in the third quarter as the Giants forged ahead 17–12. Thurman Thomas's 31-yard touchdown run in the fourth quarter gave the Bills the lead back at 19–17. Bahr's 21-yard field goal accounted for the final points of the game.

Hostetler was 20-of-32 for 222 yards. Anderson rushed the ball 21 times for 102 yards, including a 24-yarder. Dave Meggett had 9 carries for 48 yards, including a 17-yarder, and had 2 receptions for 18 yards. Mark Ingram had 5 catches for 74 yards, Mark Bavaro caught 5 passes for 50 yards, Howard Cross had 4 receptions for 39 yards, and Baker had 2 catches for 31 yards.

For Buffalo, Jim Kelly was 18-of-30 for 212 yards. He ran the ball 6 times for 23 yards. Thomas had 15 rushes for 135 yards and 5 receptions for 55 yards. Andre Reed had 8 catches for 62 yards, James Lofton caught a 61-yard pass, and Kenneth Davis had 2 receptions for 23 yards.

4. The Atlanta Falcons. Favre was a second-round draft pick in 1991 out of the University of Southern Mississippi. With the Falcons in 1991, he threw 4 passes, completing none of them, and was intercepted twice. He took one other snap, which resulted in a sack for an 11-yard loss. He was traded to the Green Bay Packers. In the second game of the 1992 season, the Packers trailed at Tampa Bay 17–0 at halftime when head coach Mike Holmgren benched starting quarterback Don Majkowski in favor of Favre, who played the second half. On his first regular-season play as a Packer, Favre threw a pass that was deflected by the Buccaneers' Ray Seals and caught by Favre. Favre was tackled and the completion went for minus 7 yards. The Packers lost 31–3.

The next week, Majkowski injured his ankle in a home game against Cincinnati, an injury severe enough that he would be out for four weeks. Favre replaced Majkowski for the remainder of the game. He fumbled 4 times during the course of the contest, a performance poor enough that the crowd chanted for Favre to be removed in favor of another Packers backup quarterback, Ty Detmer. However, down 23–17 with one minute and seven seconds left in the game, Green Bay started an offensive series on their own 8-yard line with Favre calling the signals. He completed a 42-yard pass to Sterling Sharpe. Three plays later, he threw the game-winning touchdown pass to Kitrick Taylor with 13 seconds to go in a 24–23 win.

And the rest is history.

In sixteen years with the Packers, Favre led the team to the postseason eleven times and to the Super Bowl twice—in 1996 and 1997, winning Super Bowl XXXI 35–21 over the New England Patriots. While with Green Bay, Favre passed for 4,000 yards five times and threw 30 touchdown passes eight times. He spent 2008 with the New York Jets and closed his career by playing for the Minnesota Vikings in 2009 and 2010. His 2009 season was perhaps his best ever—he was 363-of-531 for 4,202 yards with 33 touchdowns and only 7 interceptions in leading the Vikings to the brink of the Super Bowl.

Overall, Favre completed 6,300 of 10,169 passes for 71,838 yards with 508 touchdowns and 336 interceptions. He was a Pro Bowler in 1992 and 1993, from 1995 through 1997, from 2001 through 2003, and from 2007 through 2009. He was inducted into the Pro Football Hall of Fame in 2016.

5. Mark Rypien. In that 1991 season, Rypien was 249-of-421 for 3,564 yards with 28 touchdowns and 11 interceptions in leading the Redskins to a 14-2 record and the NFC Eastern Division title. In a 56–17 rout of Atlanta on November 10 that year, he was 16-of-31 for 442 yards with 6 touchdowns. A week later, on November 17 in a 41–14 win at Pittsburgh, he was 21-of-28 for 325 yards with 2 touchdowns. In a 24–7 win over the Falcons in a divisional playoff, he was 14-of-29 for 170 yards with an interception. A week later, in a 41–10 rout of Detroit in the NFC title game, he was 12-of-17 for 228 yards with 2 touchdowns. In a 37–24 triumph over the Buffalo Bills in Super Bowl XXVI at the Hubert H. Humphrey Metrodome in Minneapolis, he was 18-of-33 for 292 yards with 2 touchdowns and an interception. He threw a 10-yard touchdown pass to Earnest Byner to give the Redskins a 10–0 lead in the second quarter, and he com-

pleted a 30-yard scoring strike to Gary Clark to put them up 31–10 in the third quarter.

During his eleven-year career, which began with Washington in 1988, Rypien also played for the Cleveland Browns, St. Louis Rams, Philadelphia Eagles, and Indianapolis Colts. Overall, he completed 1,466 of 2,613 passes for 18,473 yards with 115 touchdowns and 88 interceptions. He was picked for the Pro Bowl in 1989 and 1991.

6. Buffalo Bills, Dallas Cowboys. In Super Bowl XXVII, played on January 31, 1993, at the Rose Bowl in Pasadena, California, the Cowboys defeated the Bills 52–17. The Bills took a 7–0 first-quarter lead when Thurman Thomas scored on a 2-yard run. The Cowboys tied the score on a 23-yard touchdown pass from Troy Aikman to Jay Novacek. They went ahead 14–7 after one quarter when Jimmie Jones returned a fumble 2 yards for a touchdown. Steve Christie's 21-yard field goal in the second quarter pulled Buffalo within 14–10, but the rest of the game belonged to Dallas. The Cowboys upped their lead to 28–10 at halftime on two scoring strikes from Aikman to Michael Irvin. With the score 31–17 in the fourth quarter, the Cowboys put the game away on a 45-yard touchdown pass from Aikman to Alvin Harper. They scored two more touchdowns, the second of which was a 9-yard fumble return by Ken Norton.

In Super Bowl XXVIII, played on January 30, 1994, at the Georgia Dome in Atlanta, the Cowboys beat the Bills 30–13. With Dallas leading 6–3 in the second quarter, Thomas had a 4-yard touchdown run to give Buffalo a 10–6 lead. Christie's 28-yard field goal increased the Bills' lead to 13–6 at the half. In the third quarter, James Washington returned a fumble 48 yards for a touchdown to tie the score. Emmitt Smith's 15-yard touchdown run gave the Cowboys a 20–13 lead after three quarters. Smith's 1-yard touchdown run made it 27–13, and Eddie Murray's 20-yard field goal was the game's final points.

7. Leon Lett. During a rare snow-and-sleet storm in Dallas, the Cowboys, who came into the game with a 7-3 record, were leading the 8-2 Dolphins 14–13 with fifteen seconds remaining in the game. The Dolphins sent kicker Pete Stoyanovich out to attempt a 41-yard field goal, which would likely have won the game due to how little time would have been left for the Cowboys to drive downfield after the ensuing play and subsequent kickoff. Stoyanovich's kick was blocked by Lett's line mate, Jimmie Jones, and the ball came to rest several yards away. While most of his teammates began celebrating, Lett attempted to recover the ball. He slipped as he went down, however, and knocked the ball forward. In the resulting chase for possession, the Dolphins recovered the ball in the end zone.

Had Lett simply done nothing, the play would have been whistled dead, and Dallas would have automatically received possession at the line of scrimmage. Since Lett went for the ball and touched it, though, by rule, the play was considered a muffed kick, and the Dolphins were given possession on the 1-yard line with 3 seconds left. Stoyanovich attempted an 18-yard field goal and connected as time expired, giving the Dolphins a wacky 16–14 win.

The play ultimately did not hurt the Cowboys' season as they won all of their remaining regular-season games and went on to win Super Bowl XXVIII. Conversely, the Dolphins lost the rest of their games and failed to qualify for the playoffs.

8. Tom Tupa. Tupa turned the trick in the 1994 season opener for the Cleveland Browns on September 4 at Cincinnati. With the Browns up 9–0 in the first quarter, Tupa, the holder on an extra-point attempt following Vinny Testaverde's 11-yard touchdown pass to Leroy Hoard, took the snap and ran up the middle and into the end zone to expand the Browns' lead to 11–0. In the second quarter, an 85-yard kickoff return for a touchdown by Randy Baldwin and a 92-yard punt return for a score by Eric Metcalf gave Cleveland a 25–10 halftime lead on the way to a 28–20 victory.

As for Tupa, who had 5 punts for 200 yards against the Bengals, he converted 2 more two-point conversions that year. He punted for the Browns through the next season. He also played for six other teams in a career that began in 1988 and lasted through 2004.

9. The Chiefs won 31–28. The Broncos fell to an un-Denver-like 1–5. Montana and Elway battled back and forth all night. After a scoreless first quarter, the Broncos took a 7–0 second-quarter lead on a 12-yard touchdown run by Leonard Russell. The Chiefs tied the score on Marcus Allen's 7-yard touchdown run. The Broncos took a 14–7 lead on a 27-yard touchdown pass from Elway to Anthony Miller. The Chiefs tied the score 14–14 at halftime when Montana hit J. J. Birden on a 6-yard touchdown pass. In the third quarter, Kansas City forged ahead 21–14 on a 4-yard touchdown pass from Montana to Joe Valerio. Denver tied the score after three quarters when Elway connected with Jerry Evans on a 20-yard scoring strike. Lin Elliott's 19-yard field goal with four minutes and eight seconds left gave the Chiefs a 24–21 lead. Elway ran for a 4-yard touchdown with one minute and twenty-nine seconds remaining to put the Broncos ahead 28–24. Montana, à la his days as a 49er, led a late drive to the winning score, his 5-yard touchdown pass to Willie Davis with just 8 seconds to go.

Montana was 34-of-54 for 393 yards with an interception. Allen had 16 rushes for 63 yards and 5 receptions for 49 yards. Derrick Walker had 8 catches for 98 yards, including a 23-yarder, while Davis had 7 receptions for 88 yards, including a 26-yarder. Kimble Anders had 6 catches for 56 yards, Tracy Greene caught 3 passes for 43 yards, and Birden had 2 receptions for 31 yards, including a 25-yarder.

Elway was 18-of-29 for 263 yards. He ran the ball 6 times for 38 yards. Russell had 15 carries for 41 yards. Miller had 5 receptions for 99 yards, while Glyn Milburn had 3 catches for 56 yards, including a 29-yarder. Shannon Sharpe caught 4 passes for 50 yards, and Evans had 2 receptions for 34 yards.

10. Jason Garrett. With Troy Aikman and Rodney Peete out with injuries, Garrett was thrust into the starting role for the Dallas Cowboys against Brett Favre and the Green Bay Packers at Texas Stadium in Irving. The Packers came in with a 6-5 record, and the Cowboys entered with a 9-2 mark. Garrett, whose rookie season with Dallas was the year before, led his team back from an 11-point, third-quarter deficit to a 42–31 victory.

The Packers, though, were the team that got off to a good start. They took a 7–0 first-quarter lead when Favre threw a short touchdown pass to Sterling Sharpe. The score was 10–3 in the second quarter when Favre and Sharpe hooked up again, this time on a 36-yard touchdown pass to increase the Green Bay lead to 17–3 en route to a 17–6 halftime lead. The Cowboys cut their deficit to 17–13 in the third quarter on a 5-yard touchdown run by Emmitt Smith. But Favre and Sharpe connected again, on a 30-yard scoring strike to increase the Packers' lead to 24–13. Garrett threw a 45-yard touchdown pass to Alvin Harper to pull Dallas within five points, 24–19. Daryl Johnston scored from 3 yards out to give the Cowboys their first lead at 25–24 after three quarters. Smith scored on an 18-yard run to make the score 32–24, and then Garrett hit Michael Irvin on a 35-yard touchdown pass to make it 39–24. Favre threw a 5-yard touchdown pass to Sharpe to pull the Packers within 39–31, but Chris Boniol's 35-yard field goal, his third trey of the day, accounted for the game's final points.

Garrett was 15-of-26 for 311 yards with an interception. Smith had 32 rushes for 133 yards, including a 30-yarder, and had 6 receptions for 95 yards, including a 68-yarder. Harper had 3 catches for 91 yards, Irvin caught 3 passes for 64 yards, Jay Novacek had 2 receptions for 37 yards, and Johnston had a 24-yard catch.

Favre was 27-of-40 for 257 yards. Sharpe had 9 receptions for 122 yards. Ed West had 5 catches for 36 yards,

Robert Brooks caught 3 passes for 29 yards, and Mark Chmura had 3 receptions for 28 yards.

11. The San Diego Chargers. The 1994 Chargers finished 11-5 and won the AFC Western Division title. They began the season with six straight wins. They were led by Stan Humphries, who was 264-of-453 for 3,209 yards with 17 touchdowns and 12 interceptions. Natrone Means rushed the ball 343 times for 1,350 yards with 12 touchdowns and had 39 receptions for 235 yards. Tony Martin had 50 catches for 885 yards with 7 touchdowns, while Mark Seay caught 58 passes for 645 yards with 6 touchdowns. Ronnie Harmon had 58 receptions for 615 yards with a touchdown, and Shawn Jefferson had 43 catches for 627 yards with 3 touchdowns.

The Chargers defeated the Miami Dolphins 22–21 in a divisional playoff, and they upset the Pittsburgh Steelers 17–13 in the AFC Championship game. In the Super Bowl, played on January 29, 1995, at Joe Robbie Stadium in Miami, San Francisco took a 7–0 first-quarter lead on a 44-yard touchdown pass from Steve Young to Jerry Rice. They upped their lead to 14–0 when Young hit Ricky Watters on a 51-yard scoring strike. Means scored from a yard out to cut the Chargers' deficit to 14–7 after one quarter. In the second quarter, Young threw short touchdown passes to William Floyd and Watters for a 28–7 lead. It was 28–10 at halftime. The 'Niners put the game on ice in the third quarter when Watters scored from 9 yards out and Young threw a 15-yard touchdown pass to Rice as the San Francisco lead ballooned to 42–10. The final score was 49–26.

12. The Pittsburgh Steelers and Dallas Cowboys. In 1995, the Steelers finished 11-5 in winning the AFC Central Division. They routed Buffalo in the divisional playoffs and defeated Indianapolis in a close conference title game to advance to the Super Bowl. The Cowboys were 12-4 and won the NFC Eastern Division. They beat Philadelphia in a divisional

playoff and Green Bay in the conference championship game to make it to the Super Bowl.

The Super Bowl was played on January 28, 1996, at Sun Devil Stadium in Tempe, Arizona. The Cowboys took a 10–0 lead after one quarter on a Chris Boniol 42-yard field goal and a 3-yard touchdown pass from Troy Aikman to Jay Novacek. A 35-yard field goal by Boniol upped the Cowboys' lead to 13–0. Neil O'Donnell threw a 6-yard touchdown pass to Yancey Thigpen to pull Pittsburgh within 13–7 at halftime. A short touchdown run by Emmitt Smith expanded the Cowboys' lead to 20–7 entering the fourth quarter. A 46-yard field goal by Norm Johnson and a short touchdown run by Bam Morris pulled the Steelers to within 20–17. Smith scored from 4 yards out for the game's final points in a 27–17 Dallas victory.

Aikman was 15-of-23 for 209 yards. Smith rushed the ball 18 times for 49 yards, including a 23-yarder. Michael Irvin had 5 receptions for 76 yards, Novacek had 5 catches for 50 yards, Deion Sanders caught a single pass for 47 yards, and Kevin Williams had 2 receptions for 29 yards. O'Donnell was 28-of-49 for 239 yards with 3 interceptions. Morris ran the ball 19 times for 73 yards and had 3 catches for 18 yards. Andre Hastings had 10 receptions for 98 yards, while Ernie Mills caught 8 passes for 78 yards.

13. Jacksonville lost to New England 20–6, and Carolina lost to Green Bay 30–13. The Jaguars won their last five games of the regular season to finish 9-7 and gain a wild card spot. In the team's final game of the regular season against the Atlanta Falcons, needing a win to earn a playoff berth, the Jaguars caught a bit of luck when Morten Anderson missed a 30-yard field goal with less than a minute to go that would have given the Falcons the lead. The Jags upset the Bills in Buffalo and shocked the Broncos at Denver to advance to the AFC Championship game. The Panthers were 12-4 and won the NFC Western Division title. They beat Dallas in a

divisional playoff, which earned them a spot in the conference championship game.

In the Jaguars–Patriots AFC title tilt at New England, the Patriots took a 7–0 first-quarter lead when Curtis Martin scored on a 1-yard touchdown run. Two field goals each by the Patriots' Adam Vinatieri and the Jaguars' Mike Hollis resulted in a 13–6 Pats' lead in the fourth quarter. Otis Smith returned a fumble 47 yards for a touchdown and the game's final points.

In the Panthers–Packers NFC Championship game in Green Bay, the Panthers took a 7–0 lead after one quarter on a 3-yard touchdown pass from Kerry Collins to Howard Griffith. The Packers tied the score in the second quarter when Brett Favre completed a 29-yard touchdown pass to Dorsey Levens. John Kasay kicked a 22-yard field goal as Carolina forged ahead 10–7, but Antonio Freeman's 6-yard touchdown catch from Favre gave the lead back to Green Bay 14–10. In the third quarter, with the Packers up 20–13, Edgar Bennett scored from 4 yards out to increase the lead to 27–13 entering the fourth quarter. Chris Jacke's 28-yard field goal was the game's final points.

14. The Green Bay Packers and Atlanta Falcons. Denver defeated Green Bay 31–24 in Super Bowl XXXII, played on January 25, 1998, at Qualcomm Stadium in San Diego. The Packers took a 7–0 first-quarter lead on a 22-yard touchdown pass from Brett Favre to Antonio Freeman. Short touchdown runs by Terrell Davis and John Elway and a 51-yard field goal by Jason Elam had the Broncos up 17–7 in the second quarter. The Packers pulled to within 17–14 at halftime on a 6-yard touchdown pass from Favre to Mark Chmura. They tied the score in the third quarter on a 27-yard Ryan Longwell field goal. The Broncos went up 24–17 entering the fourth quarter when Davis scored on a 1-yard run. Favre and Freeman hooked up again, this time on a 13-yard scoring strike, to tie the score 24–24. Davis's 1-yard run for a touchdown was the game's final points.

The Broncos beat Atlanta 34–19 in Super Bowl XXXIII, played on January 31, 1999, at Pro Player Stadium in Miami. The Falcons took a 3–0 first-quarter lead on a 32-yard field goal by Morten Andersen. The Broncos forged ahead 7–3 after one quarter on a 1-yard touchdown run by Howard Griffith. In the second quarter, Elam's 26-yard field goal and an 80-yard touchdown pass from Elway to Rod Smith increased the Denver lead to 17–3. Andersen's 28-yard field goal made it 17–6 at the half. Griffith had another 1-yard touchdown run in the fourth quarter for a 24–6 Denver lead. Elway scored from 3 yards out as the Broncos' advantage ballooned to 31–6. Tim Dwight returned the ensuing kickoff 94 yards for a touchdown to make it 31–13, but it was way too little, too late as the Broncos put it in cruise control the rest of the way.

15. c. 1996, 1997, 1998. On June 12, 1996, the city of Cleveland and the NFL announced terms of a historic public-private partnership that would continue the Browns franchise and guarantee a new state-of-the-art stadium in Cleveland in 1999. At a league meeting in Orlando, Florida, on March 23, 1998, NFL owners agreed that the Cleveland Browns would be an expansion team in 1999. The NFL awarded majority ownership of the franchise to Al Lerner on September 8, 1998. The Browns did not have much time, but they spent months putting together a team through free agency, the expansion draft, and the regular draft in time for the 1999 season.

The Browns finished 2-14 in 1999 and 3-13 in 2000. They improved to 7-9 in 2001 and 9-7 and a playoff berth in 2002. Ever since then, though, for the most part, it has been a nightmare for the Browns and their fans with just one winning season. However, things seem to be headed in the right direction now.

16. Tim Couch. Couch in 1999 was 223-of-399 for 2,447 yards with 15 touchdowns and 13 interceptions, becoming only the sixth rookie quarterback in the NFL since 1952 to

have more touchdown passes than interceptions. He left the December 19 home game against the Jaguars with an ankle sprain, causing him to miss the final game of the season against the Colts. After getting off to a good start in 2000, Couch played in just seven games that year after fracturing his right thumb in a practice session on October 19. In 2001, he came back strong by going 272-of-454 for 3,040 yards with 17 touchdowns and 21 interceptions.

In 2002, Couch missed the first two games due to a preseason injury. He led the Browns to a playoff berth, including several late-game comebacks. He played only part of the regular-season finale against Atlanta due to another injury. The injury kept him out of the Browns' wild card playoff loss to Pittsburgh. His final season with Cleveland was in 2003. He was released after the season. He tried to catch on with a handful of other teams during the next four years, but an arm injury forced him to retire. Overall, he completed 1,025 of 1,714 passes for 11,131 yards with 64 touchdowns and 67 interceptions. Most Browns fans would be shocked to learn that he has the highest career completion percentage in team history at 59.8 (minimum 750 passes).

17. Brett Favre   "Gunslinger"
Randall Cunningham   "The Ultimate Weapon"
Richard Dent   "Sackman"
Neal Anderson   "Charley"
Andre Rison   "Bad Mood"
Reggie White   "The Minister of Defense"
Deion Sanders   "Prime Time"
Rod Woodson   "Woody"
Ricky Watters   "Thunder"
Desmond Howard   "Magic"

18. Orlando Brown. A right tackle, Brown was the center of attention in one of the more unusual plays in NFL history when he was hit in his open right eye with a penalty flag weighted with ball bearings thrown by referee Jeff Triplette. This happened during the second quarter of a home game against the Jacksonville Jaguars in the second-to-last game of the season. Triplette immediately apologized to Brown. Brown left the game temporarily, then returned to the field only to shove Triplette, knocking him to the ground. Brown was ejected from the game and had to be escorted off the field by his teammates. He was subsequently suspended by the NFL, but the suspension was shortened to one game—the season finale against Indianapolis—when the severity of his injury became apparent.

Brown's eye suffered direct trauma that affected his vision and could have developed into glaucoma. He was cut by the Browns in September 2000. At the time, he had a six-year $27 million contract from which he collected a $7.5 million signing bonus. He sat out the entire 2000 season waiting for his eye to heal. In fact, he suffered from temporary blindness. In 2001, he filed a $200 million lawsuit against the NFL. U.S. District Judge Gerard E. Lynch ruled on March 18, 2002, that the NFL could not force the lawsuit into arbitration by saying that a union contract governs a player's claim that his career was ruined. Later in 2002, Brown settled for a sum between $15 million and $25 million. Brown, who actually began his career with the original Browns in 1994 and 1995 and played for Baltimore from 1996 through 1998, returned to the NFL and spent 2003 through 2005 with the Ravens.

19. The Buffalo Bills. The controversial play occurred toward the end of an AFC Wild Card Playoff game at Adelphia Coliseum in Nashville, Tennessee. The Bills had taken a 16–15 lead on a field goal with sixteen seconds left. On the ensuing kickoff return, Frank Wycheck threw a lateral pass

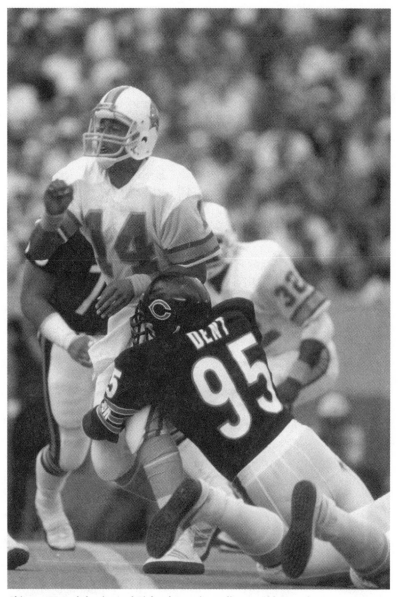

Chicago Bears defensive end Richard Dent is a split second late to the Tampa Bay quarterback.

Jerry Coli/Dreamstime.com

across the field to Kevin Dyson, who then ran 75 yards to score the winning touchdown in a 22–16 Tennessee victory. The play began when Steve Christie kicked a high and short pooch that was fielded by Lorenzo Neal. Neal handed the ball to Wycheck, who had been behind him and nearly ran into him. This formed the key shift in the play—the Bills chased Wycheck to the right side of the field, breaking their lanes in the process. Wycheck then threw the ball across the field to Dyson. As Dyson caught the ball, the momentum of the play abruptly went to the left and caught every Bills player except for Christie out of position. Dyson thus had an open path in front of him and ran all the way for a touchdown. The Titans made one final kickoff, and the clock expired during the Bills' return.

20. a. Tennessee Titans. In 1999, the Titans finished 13-3 and earned an AFC Wild Card Playoff berth. They defeated Buffalo, Indianapolis, and Jacksonville in the playoffs to advance to the Super Bowl. The Rams were also 13-3 in winning the NFC Western Division title. They beat Minnesota and Tampa Bay in the playoffs to reach the Super Bowl.

The Super Bowl was played on January 30, 2000, at the Georgia Dome in Atlanta. Three Jeff Wilkins field goals had St. Louis in front 9–0 at halftime. In the third quarter, Kurt Warner threw a 9-yard touchdown pass to Torry Holt to increase the Rams' lead to 16–0. Two short Eddie George touchdown runs pulled the Titans to within 16–13 in the fourth quarter. With two minutes and twelve seconds left, Al Del Greco kicked a 43-yard field goal to tie the score. On the ensuing drive, Warner completed a 73-yard touchdown pass to Isaac Bruce as the Rams regained the lead 23–16 with one minute and fifty-four seconds to go. The Titans then drove to the St. Louis 10-yard line with 6 seconds left, but on the final play of the game, Rams linebacker Mike Jones tackled Tennessee wide receiver Kevin Dyson, who had caught a pass from Steve McNair, 1 yard short of the goal line to prevent a potential game-tying touchdown.

Kurt Warner
Jerry Coli/Dreamstime.com

Warner was 24-of-45 for 414 yards. Bruce had 6 receptions for 162 yards, Holt had 7 catches for 109 yards, including a 32-yarder, and Marshall Faulk caught 5 passes for 90 yards, including a 52-yarder. McNair was 22-of-36 for 214 yards. He ran the ball 8 times for 64 yards, including a 23-yarder. George had 28 rushes for 95 yards and 2 receptions for 35 yards, including a 32-yarder. Jackie Harris had 7 catches for 64 yards, Dyson caught 4 passes for 41 yards, and Wycheck had 5 receptions for 35 yards.

THE 2000s

PRO FOOTBALL IN A NEW MILLENNIUM

The 2000s brought Super Bowls in February and champion-ships to Tampa Bay and New Orleans, two cities that, for a long time, no one ever thought would celebrate Super Bowl titles. The decade also brought the closest thing to a dynasty, the New England Patriots, and out-of-this-world numbers in the passing game from Tom Brady, Carson Palmer, and Eli Manning, Pey-ton's younger brother, to name a few.

QUESTIONS

1. What San Francisco 49ers quarterback passed for 4,278 yards with 31 touchdowns and 10 interceptions in 2000? *Answer on page 186.*

2. What team beat the New York Giants 34–7 in Super Bowl XXXV? *Answer on page 188.*

3. The bizarre "Bottlegate" incident on December 16, 2001, in which angry Cleveland Browns fans threw thousands of plastic bottles from the Cleveland Browns Stadium stands, in response to what they believed to be a terrible officiating call, occurred during a 15–10 loss to what current AFC South team? *Answer on page 188.*

4. What two teams played in the infamous "Tuck Rule Game"? *Answer on page 190.*

5. What two teams opposed one another in the first-ever Super Bowl played in February? *Answer on page 190.*

6. What running back led the NFL with 1,853 rushing yards in 2002? *Answer on page 191.*

   a. LaDainian Tomlinson   **b.** Priest Holmes
   c. Clinton Portis   **d.** Ricky Williams

7. _____, a former backup to Peyton Manning in Indianapolis, came out of nowhere to lead the Cleveland Browns to two regular-season wins and a remarkable performance in a near-miss playoff loss to Pittsburgh on January 5, 2003. *Answer on page 192.*

8. The Tampa Bay Buccaneers defeated the Denver Broncos in Super Bowl XXXVII. True or false? *Answer on page 193.*

9. Who returned two kickoffs and two punts for touchdowns in 2003? *Answer on page 193.*

   a. Wes Welker   **b.** Dante Hall
   c. Brian Mitchell   **d.** Josh Scobey

10. The New England Patriots defeated the _____ in Super Bowl XXXVIII and the _____ in Super Bowl XXXIX. *Answer on page 194.*

11. What AFC North Division safety led the NFL in 2004 with 9 interceptions and 358 interception return yards? *Answer on page 195.*

12. What NFC South wide receiver led the NFL with 103 receptions, 1,563 receiving yards, and 12 touchdown catches in 2005? *Answer on page 196.*

13. What head coach was fired after leading his team to a 14-2 record—the best in the NFL—in 2006? *Answer on page 198.*

14. The Patriots' Tom Brady and the Colts' Peyton Manning had many duels against one another throughout their careers. Perhaps the most memorable occurred in the AFC Championship game on January 21, 2007, at the RCA Dome in Indianapolis. The Colts recovered from a 21–3 second-quarter deficit to defeat the Patriots. What was the final score? *Answer on page 198.*

   a. 38–34
   b. 37–31
   c. 31–28
   d. 34–30

15. When the New England Patriots finished 16-0 in 2007, their points total broke a nine-year-old record. How many points did the Patriots score? *Answer on page 199.*

   a. 579   b. 589
   c. 599   d. 609

16. What two AFC North teams opposed one another in the unforgettable "Ricochet" game on November 18, 2007? *Answer on page 200.*

17. What NFC West team came out of nowhere to advance all the way to Super Bowl XLIII? *Answer on page 201.*

18. What wide receiver led the NFL in receiving yards in 2008 and 2009? *Answer on page 202.*

19. What Cleveland Brown returned two kickoffs for touchdowns in a 41–34 Browns' victory over the Chiefs in Kansas City on December 20, 2009? *Answer on page 203.*

20. The New Orleans Saints defeated the _____ 31–17 in Super Bowl XLIV. *Answer on page 203.*

   a. Pittsburgh Steelers
   b. Indianapolis Colts
   c. Denver Broncos
   d. New England Patriots

ANSWERS

1. Jeff Garcia. That season, Garcia had a stretch in which he had 4 touchdown passes and no interceptions three times in four weeks. Unfortunately for Garcia and the 49ers, they lost two of those games. The first was a 41–24 victory over Dallas on September 24 in which he was 16-of-26 for 178 yards. The second was a 34–28 overtime loss to Oakland on October 8 in which he was 28-of-41 for 336 yards. The third was a 42–27 loss to Green Bay on October 15 in which he was 27-of-42 for 336 yards. Garcia also ran the ball 72 times

for 414 yards with 4 touchdowns. The 'Niners finished just 6–10 that season.

Garcia went undrafted in 1999 out of San Jose State University but was signed by the 49ers as a free agent. He had a decent rookie season that year. In 2001, he led San Francisco to a 12-4 record and a playoff berth. That year, he was 316-of-504 for 3,538 yards with 32 touchdowns and 12 interceptions. He ran the ball 72 times for 254 yards with 5 touchdowns. He had two games in which he passed for 4 touchdowns and no interceptions. The first was a 28–27 win over New Orleans on November 11 in which he was 21-of-34 for 252 yards. The second was a regular season–ending 38–0 win over the same Saints in which he was 14-of-21 for 263 yards. The next season, he directed the 49ers to a 10-6 record and the NFC West Division crown. He was 328-of-528 for 3,344 yards with 21 touchdowns and 10 interceptions. He ran the ball 73 times for 353 yards with 3 touchdowns. In a memorable 39–38 wild card playoff win over the New York Giants in which the 49ers erased a twenty-four-point deficit, he was 27-of-44 for 331 yards with 3 touchdowns and an interception.

After spending one more season with San Francisco, 2004 with Cleveland, and 2005 with Detroit, Garcia helped Philadelphia to a 10-6 record and the NFC East Division title in 2006 after starter Donovan McNabb was lost for the season to a knee injury on November 19. Garcia threw 10 touchdown passes and only 2 picks. In a 23–20 wild card playoff win over the Giants, he was 17-of-31 for 153 yards with a touchdown. He spent 2007 and 2008 with Tampa Bay, leading the 2007 Buccaneers to a 9-7 record and the NFC South Division title. That year, he had 13 touchdown passes and just 4 interceptions. He ended his career back in Philadelphia in 2009.

Overall, Garcia completed 2,264 of 3,676 passes for 25,537 yards with 161 touchdowns and 83 interceptions. He ran the ball 468 times for 2,140 yards with 26 touchdowns. He was a Pro Bowler from 2000 through 2002 and in 2007.

2. The Baltimore Ravens. The 2000 Ravens' defense is considered to be one of the greatest of all time. It was led by Ray Lewis, Rod Woodson, Duane Starks, and Chris McAlister. The Ravens finished 12-4 and in second place in the AFC Central Division. They shut out four opponents and held opponents to fewer than 10 points nine times. In the postseason, they beat Denver 21–3, Tennessee 24–10, and Oakland 16–3 en route to the Super Bowl.

The Super Bowl was played on January 28, 2001, at Raymond James Stadium in Tampa, Florida. The Ravens took a 7–0 lead after one quarter on a 38-yard touchdown pass from Trent Dilfer to Brandon Stokley. They upped their lead to 10–0 at halftime on a 47-yard field goal by Matt Stover. In the third quarter, Starks returned an interception 49 yards for a touchdown to make the score 17–0. Ron Dixon returned the ensuing kickoff 97 yards for a touchdown to pull the Giants within 17–7. Incredibly, Jermaine Lewis returned *that* ensuing kickoff 84 yards for a touchdown for a 24–7 Baltimore lead entering the fourth quarter. The Ravens put the game away with eight minutes and forty-five seconds to go on a 3-yard touchdown run by Jamal Lewis to increase their lead to 31–7. For good measure, Stover kicked a 34-yard field goal for the game's final points. The Ravens limited the Giants to just 152 total yards and 11 first downs.

3. The Jacksonville Jaguars. The Browns, still in playoff contention, were losing by five points and had the ball deep in Jaguars territory late in the game. On fourth down, Tim Couch passed the ball to Quincy Morgan, who struggled to hold onto the ball after getting hit by safety James Boyd. Morgan lost the ball temporarily when he hit the ground but recovered his own fumble, which would have made it a catch and given the Browns a first down. That would have allowed them time for four tries to get into the end zone. Couch quickly spiked the ball to stop the clock, which, by rule, ends the option for an instant-replay challenge. Referee Terry McAulay, though, ruled that the replay buzzer on his belt went off before the snap.

Ray Lewis
Jerry Coli/Dreamstime.com

Jacksonville's request for a review was honored, and the ruling of a completion was overturned, provoking the bottle-throwing escapade. Due to the danger it presented, McAulay ruled the game over and ordered both teams to their respective locker rooms with forty-eight seconds still left on the clock. Nearly a half hour later, however, both sides returned to the field for one last snap to officially complete the game via orders from NFL commissioner Paul Tagliabue.

4. The Oakland Raiders and New England Patriots. It was an AFC Divisional Playoff on January 19, 2002, at Foxboro Stadium in Foxboro, Massachusetts. The name "Tuck Rule Game" originated from a controversial game-changing play. With Oakland leading 13–10 late in the fourth quarter, Raiders cornerback Charles Woodson sacked Tom Brady, which in turn, initially appeared to cause a fumble that was eventually recovered by Raiders linebacker Greg Biekert. If it was indeed a fumble, it would have almost certainly sealed the game for Oakland.

Officials reviewed the play, though, and eventually determined that even though Brady had seemingly halted his passing motion and was attempting to "tuck" the ball back into his body, it was an incomplete pass and not a fumble under the then-effective NFL rules. As a result, the original call was overturned, and the ball was given back to the Patriots, who subsequently moved the ball into field-goal range. With 27 seconds left, Adam Vinatieri kicked a 45-yard field goal to tie the game 13–13, and it went into overtime. In the extra session, Vinatieri booted a 23-yard field goal to give the Patriots a 16–13 victory.

5. The New England Patriots and St. Louis Rams. They played one another in Super Bowl XXXVI on February 3, 2002, at the Louisiana Superdome in New Orleans. The Patriots finished 11-5 and won the AFC Eastern Division. They beat Oakland and Pittsburgh in the playoffs en route to the Super Bowl. The Rams, known at the time as "The Greatest Show on Turf" because of their explosive offense, were 14-2 in win-

ning the NFC Western Division. In the playoffs, they defeated Green Bay and Philadelphia to advance to the Super Bowl.

In the Super Bowl, the Rams took a 3–0 lead after the first quarter on a 50-yard field goal by Jeff Wilkins. The Patriots forged ahead 7–3 in the second quarter when Ty Law returned an interception 47 yards for a touchdown. The Pats upped their lead to 14–3 at halftime on an 8-yard touchdown pass from Tom Brady to David Patten. A 37-yard field goal by Adam Vinatieri made the score 17–3 entering the fourth quarter. Kurt Warner's 2-yard touchdown run cut the Rams' deficit to 17–10. With one minute and thirty seconds remaining, Warner threw a 26-yard touchdown pass to Ricky Proehl to tie the score. With no time-outs left, Brady drove his team down the field. Vinatieri kicked a 48-yard field goal as time expired, giving New England a thrilling 20–17 victory. It remains the only time in Super Bowl history that a game was won by a score on the final play.

6. d. Ricky Williams. Williams accomplished the feat in his first season with the Miami Dolphins after spending his first three seasons, 1999 through 2001, with the New Orleans Saints. Williams also led the league in 2002 with 383 rushing attempts. He had 16 rushing touchdowns. He also had 47 receptions for 363 yards with a touchdown. He had ten games in which he ran for 100 yards. He really started pouring it on late in the season. Despite a 38–21 loss to Buffalo on December 1, he had 27 rushes for 228 yards with 2 touchdowns. The next week, in a 27–9 win over Chicago on December 9, he ran the ball 31 times for 216 yards with 2 touchdowns. In a season-ending 27–24 overtime defeat to New England, he rushed for 185 yards on 31 carries with 2 touchdowns.

In 1999, the Saints traded eight draft picks over two seasons, including two first-rounders, to the Washington Redskins so they could move up from their own number twelve position in the draft to the number five spot. In his rookie season with the Saints that year, Williams rushed the ball 253 times for 884 yards with 2 touchdowns and had 28 receptions for 172 yards. In 2000, he had 248 rushes for 1,000 yards with 8 touchdowns and had 44 catches for 409 yards with a touchdown. The next season, he ran the ball 313 times for 1,245 yards with 6 touchdowns and caught 60 passes for 511 yards with a touchdown. In 2003, with the Dolphins, he had an NFL-high 392 carries for 1,372 yards with 9 touchdowns and had 50 receptions for 351 yards with a touchdown.

Off-the-field issues caused Williams's numbers to drop, for the most part, throughout the remainder of his career. He was with Miami through 2010 but missed the entire 2004 and 2006 seasons. He did rush for 1,121 yards on 241 carries with 11 touchdowns in 2009. He concluded his career in 2011 with Baltimore. He helped lead three teams to the postseason—the Saints in 2000, the Dolphins in 2008, and the Ravens in 2011.

Overall, Williams had 2,431 rushes for 10,009 yards with 66 touchdowns and had 342 receptions for 2,606 yards with 8 touchdowns. He was a Pro Bowler in 2002.

7. Kelly Holcomb. After backing up Manning in 1997, Holcomb backed up Tim Couch in 2001 and started the first two games in 2002 after Couch was injured during the preseason. In those two games, Holcomb put up impressive numbers against Kansas City and Cincinnati. He replaced an injured Couch again in the season finale and helped the Browns to a win over the visiting Atlanta Falcons that, in the end, put them in the playoffs. In a 36–33 loss at Pittsburgh in a wild card game, Holcomb was 26-of-43 for 429 yards with 3 touchdowns and an interception.

Holcomb beat out Couch for the starting job in 2003, but he was just not consistent enough to hold on to it. He and Couch each started eight games, but neither could really get much going during a 5-11 season. Holcomb did have his moments, though. He was 29-of-35 for 392 yards with 3 touchdowns in a 44–6 rout of Arizona on November 16 that season. On November 28, 2004, he was 30-of-39 for 413 yards with 5 touchdowns and 2 interceptions in a 58–48 loss at Cincinnati.

The 2004 season was Holcomb's last in Cleveland. He went on to play for Buffalo in 2005 and Minnesota in 2007.

Overall, Holcomb completed 565 of 893 passes for 5,916 yards with 39 touchdowns and 38 interceptions.

8. False. They beat the Oakland Raiders. Tampa Bay was a terrible team, for the most part, in their first twenty-one seasons from 1976 through 1996. From 1997 through 2001, the Buccaneers qualified for the playoffs every year but one. Then in 2002 under new head coach Jon Gruden, they finished a franchise-best 12-4 and won the NFC South Division title. They won with ease over San Francisco and Philadelphia in the playoffs to reach the Super Bowl. Oakland was 11-5 in winning the AFC West Division title. The Raiders easily defeated the Jets and Titans in the playoffs to advance to the Super Bowl.

The Super Bowl was played on January 26, 2003, at Qualcomm Stadium in San Diego. With the Buccaneers leading 6–3 in the second quarter, Mike Alstott rushed for a 2-yard touchdown to give them a 13–3 lead. Two touchdown passes from Brad Johnson to Keenan McCardell had Tampa Bay up 27–3 in the third quarter. Later in the third, Dwight Smith returned an interception 44 yards for a touchdown to increase the Tampa Bay lead to 34–3. With six minutes and six seconds left in the game, Jerry Rice caught a 48-yard touchdown pass from Rich Gannon to pull the Raiders within 34–21. With one minute and eighteen seconds to go, Derrick Brooks returned an interception 44 yards for a touchdown to expand the Buccaneers' lead to 41–21 and nail the coffin door shut on the Raiders. For good measure, Smith had his second pick-six of the game, a 50-yarder, with two seconds to go to give the Bucs a 48–21 victory.

9. b. Dante Hall. Hall achieved the feat with a return touchdown in four straight weeks. During a 41–20 win over Pittsburgh on September 14, he returned a kickoff 100 yards for a touchdown. In a 42–14 victory over Houston on September 21, he returned a punt 73 yards for a touchdown. During a 17–10 win over Baltimore on September 28, he returned a

kickoff 97 yards for the winning score. In a 24–23 win over Denver on October 5, he returned a punt 93 yards, again for the winning score.

Hall, whose rookie season with Kansas City was in 2000, had 3 returns for touchdowns in 2002—2 on punts and 1 on a kickoff. And he did it all in a two-week stretch. During a 49–0 win over Arizona on December 1, he returned a punt 90 yards for a touchdown. In a 49–10 win over St. Louis on December 8, he returned a kickoff 88 yards for a touchdown and returned a punt 86 yards for a touchdown. In 2004, he returned 2 kickoffs for touchdowns, and in 2005 he returned 1 kickoff for a touchdown. In 2006, he returned a punt for a touchdown. He returned one last punt for a score in 2007 as a member of the St. Louis Rams. He played with the Rams through 2008. He also had 1 kick-off return for a touchdown in the postseason, a 92-yarder during a 38–31 defeat to Indianapolis in an AFC Divisional Playoff on January 11, 2004.

Overall in his career, Hall returned 6 punts and 6 kickoffs for touchdowns.

10. Carolina Panthers, Philadelphia Eagles. The Patriots beat the Panthers 32–29 in Super Bowl XXXVIII on February 1, 2004, at Reliant Stadium in Houston. They beat the Eagles 24–21 in Super Bowl XXXIX on February 6, 2005, at Alltel Stadium in Jacksonville, Florida.

In Super Bowl XXXVIII, after a scoreless first quarter, the Patriots took a 7–0 second-quarter lead when Tom Brady completed a 5-yard touchdown pass to Deion Branch. The Panthers tied the score late in the first half on a 39-yard touchdown pass from Jake Delhomme to Steve Smith. New England forged back ahead 14–7 on a 5-yard touchdown pass from Brady to David Givens. John Kasay's 50-yard field goal at the end of the half pulled the Panthers to within 14–10. The score stayed the same until early in the fourth quarter when Antowain Smith scored on a 2-yard run to up the Patriots' lead to 21–10. Carolina took its only lead,

22–21, on a 33-yard touchdown run by DeShaun Foster and an 85-yard touchdown pass from Delhomme to Muhsin Muhammad. With two minutes and fifty-one seconds remaining, Mike Vrabel caught a short touchdown pass from Brady as the Patriots took back the lead 29–22. With one minute and eight seconds to go, Ricky Proehl caught a 12-yard touchdown pass from Delhomme to tie the score at 29. Kasay's ensuing kickoff went out of bounds, giving New England the ball on their own 40-yard line. Brady drove the Patriots to Adam Vinatieri's 41-yard field goal with 4 seconds left for the final points of the game.

In Super Bowl XXXIX, the Eagles took a 7–0 second-quarter lead on a 6-yard touchdown pass from Donovan McNabb to L. J. Smith. The Patriots tied the score at halftime when Brady threw a 4-yard touchdown pass to Givens. With the score 14–14 early in the fourth quarter, Corey Dillon scored from 2 yards out for a 21–14 New England lead. With eight minutes and forty seconds to go, Vinatieri booted a 22-yard field goal to expand the Patriots' lead to 24–14. McNabb hit Greg Lewis on a 30-yard touchdown pass to pull the Eagles within three points with one minute and forty-eight seconds to go, but that was as close as they got.

11. Ed Reed. Reed did it as a member of the Baltimore Ravens, with whom he played his rookie season in 2002. In 2004, he had a 2-interception game in a 23–9 victory over Cincinnati on September 26. On November 7, he returned an interception 106 yards for the clinching touchdown with twenty-seven seconds to go in a 27–13 win over Cleveland. The next week, on November 14 in a 20–17 win over the Jets, he returned an interception 78 yards. The season before, in 2003, he had 7 interceptions, including a 54-yard pick-six on the final play of the game in a 33–13 victory over the Browns on September 14.

In 2008, Reed had a league-best 9 interceptions and 264 interception return yards. He had 2 picks in a game four times—during a 36–7 win over Philadelphia on November

23, in a 24–10 victory over Washington on December 7, during a 33–24 win over Dallas on December 20, and in a 27–7 triumph over Jacksonville the very next week on December 28 in the regular-season finale. He had two pick-sixes that year, the first a 32-yarder during a 28–10 victory over the Browns on September 21 and the second a 107-yarder in the win over the Eagles. He also returned a fumble 22 yards for a touchdown in a 24–10 win over Washington on December 7. In 2010, he had both an NFL-leading 8 interceptions and 183 interception return yards. He had three games in which he had 2 picks that year—a 37–34 overtime victory against Buffalo on October 24, a 20–10 win over Cleveland on December 26, and a 13–7 triumph over Cincinnati on January 2, 2011. He played with the Ravens through 2012 and spent 2013 with Houston and the New York Jets.

Overall, Reed had 64 interceptions and 1,590 interception return yards. He returned 7 interceptions for touchdowns. In the postseason, he totaled 9 interceptions and 168 interception return yards. His lone playoff pick-six was a 64-yarder during a 27–9 victory over Miami in an AFC Wild Card Playoff game on January 4, 2009.

12. Steve Smith. He achieved the feat as a member of the Carolina Panthers. In a 27–24 loss to Miami on September 25, he had 11 receptions for 170 yards with 3 touchdowns. In a 38–13 win over Minnesota on October 30, he had 11 catches for 201 yards with a touchdown. In a 13–3 defeat to Chicago on November 20, he caught 14 passes for 169 yards. That season, he led the Panthers to an 11-5 record and a playoff berth. In a 23–0 victory over the New York Giants in an NFC Wild Card Playoff game, he had 10 receptions for 84 yards with a touchdown and also scored on a 12-yard run. In a 29–21 divisional playoff win over the Bears, he had 12 catches for 218 yards with 2 touchdowns for 58 and 39 yards.

Smith, whose rookie season with Carolina was in 2001, helped the 2003 Panthers to an 11-5 record and the NFC South Division title. The Panthers advanced all the way to Super Bowl XXXVIII. That season, Smith had 88 receptions for 1,110 yards with 7 touchdowns. In a 29–10 wild card win over Dallas, he had 5 receptions for 135 yards, including a 70-yarder, with a touchdown. In a 29–23 double-overtime victory against St. Louis in a divisional playoff, he caught 6 passes for 163 yards, including a 69-yarder for the winning score. In a 32–29 loss to New England in the Super Bowl, he had 4 receptions for 80 yards, including a 39-yarder for his team's first touchdown.

Smith also eclipsed a thousand receiving yards with Carolina from 2006 through 2008 and in 2011 and 2012. He did it in 2014 with the Baltimore Ravens, for whom he played from that season through 2016. He helped the Panthers advance to the postseason in 2008 and 2013. He helped the Ravens to the playoffs in 2014. In a 30–17 wild card playoff win over Pittsburgh that season, he had 5 catches for 101 yards, including a 40-yarder.

Overall, Smith had 1,031 receptions for 14,731 yards with 81 touchdowns. He was a Pro Bowler in 2001, 2005, 2006, 2008, and 2011.

13. Marty Schottenheimer. Schottenheimer was relieved of his duties after his San Diego Chargers had that remarkable season, his last as a head coach. Reasons for his firing included a strained relationship with general manager A. J. Smith, which reached a breaking point when four assistants left for positions with other teams. These coaches all left to pursue higher-level opportunities, which cannot be prevented by the team they are leaving under NFL rules. Two of them became head coaches instead of merely making a lateral move to the same position with another team.

In five seasons with the Chargers, Schottenheimer led them to three winning records and two playoff berths. Both resulted in first-game defeats—to the Jets in 2004 and to the Patriots in 2006. Overall with the Chargers, he had a record of 47-33. Going back to his days as head coach of the Kansas City Chiefs and Cleveland Browns (he was also Washington's head coach for a season), Schottenheimer had never had much success in the playoffs. Although he led the Browns to two AFC Championship games and the Chiefs to one, in addition to leading both teams to multiple other postseason appearances, his all-time playoff record was just 5-13. His overall regular-season record was 200-126-1.

14. a. 38–34. Heading into the game, Manning's Colts were on a two-game winning streak against Brady's Patriots, having beaten them earlier during that 2006 season and in the 2005 season. Prior to that, Brady's Pats had won the first six meetings, two of which were postseason games—one AFC title game and one divisional playoff contest. In 2006, the Patriots and Colts both finished 12-4, the Pats winning the AFC East Division and the Colts winning the AFC South Division. In the playoffs, New England defeated the New York Jets and San Diego to reach the conference championship game. Indianapolis beat Kansas City and Baltimore to advance to the conference title game.

In the AFC Championship game, the Patriots took a 7–0 first-quarter lead when Logan Mankins recovered a fumble by a teammate in the end zone for a touchdown. With New England up 7–3 in the second quarter, Corey Dillon ran for a 7-yard touchdown to increase the lead to 14–3. Less than a minute later, Asante Samuel returned an interception off a pass by Manning 39 yards for a touchdown and a 21–3 Patriots' lead. It was 21–6 at halftime. In the third quarter, Manning ran for a 1-yard touchdown to pull the Colts within 21–13. Less than four minutes later, he threw a short touchdown pass to Dan Klecko, which tied the score 21–21. Brady's 6-yard touchdown pass to Jabar Gaffney gave the Patriots the lead again, 28–21 entering the fourth quarter. Jeff Saturday recovered a teammate's fumble in the end zone for a touchdown as Indianapolis tied the score again at

28–28. Stephen Gostkowski's 28-yard field goal put the Pats back on top 31–28. A couple of minutes later, Adam Vinatieri tied the score with a 36-yard field goal. With three minutes and forty-nine seconds remaining, Gostkowski booted a 43-yard field goal to give New England the lead again, 34–31. Joseph Addai's 3-yard touchdown run with a minute left accounted for the winning points. The Colts went on to defeat the Chicago Bears 29–17 in Super Bowl XLI.

Brady's Patriots won two of the next three meetings with Manning's Colts through 2010. After sitting out the 2011 season with an injury, Manning joined the Denver Broncos in 2012. His Broncos and Brady's Patriots faced each other five times through 2016, Manning's final season. During that time, New England won the three regular-season meetings, and Denver won the other two games, both of which were AFC title contests.

Overall, including the postseason, Brady won the head-to-head series with Manning 11–6.

15. b. 589. The Patriots' record has since been broken, by the 2013 Denver Broncos, who amassed 606 points. The 2007 Patriots yielded 274 points. They were an offensive machine, scoring 31 points or more twelve times and hanging up 48 points or more four times, including three weeks in a row in October—48–27 over Dallas, 49–28 over Miami, and 52–7 over Washington.

Tom Brady was 398-of-578 for 4,806 yards with 50 touchdowns and 8 interceptions. Laurence Maroney rushed the ball 185 times for 835 yards with 6 touchdowns. Wes Welker had an NFL-best 112 receptions for 1,175 yards with 8 touchdowns, while Randy Moss had 98 catches for 1,493 yards with a league-leading 23 touchdowns.

New England defeated Jacksonville 31–20 and San Diego 21–12 in the playoffs. In Super Bowl XLII, played on February 3, 2008, at the University of Phoenix Stadium in Glendale, Arizona, the Patriots' run for a 19-0 season fell one step short in a 17–14 upset loss to the New York Giants. Lawrence Tynes kicked a 32-yard field goal to give the Giants a 3–0 lead after one quarter. Maroney's 1-yard touchdown run put the Patriots on top 7–3 at halftime. The score stayed the same until the fourth quarter when Eli Manning's 5-yard touchdown pass to David Tyree gave New York a 10–7 lead. The Patriots seemed to have won the game when, with two minutes and forty-two seconds left, Brady completed a 6-yard touchdown pass to Moss for a 14–10 New England lead. Manning, though, drove his team down the field to the winning touchdown, a 13-yard pass to Plaxico Burress with thirty-five seconds to go. The 1972 Miami Dolphins thus remain the only NFL team to finish a season undefeated, including the postseason.

16. The Cleveland Browns and Baltimore Ravens. What happened at the end of regulation in this game at M&T Bank Stadium in Baltimore was truly remarkable. The Browns were 5-4 and needed a win to keep realistic playoff hopes. The Ravens were 4-5, and their playoff hopes were in even bigger jeopardy. The Browns had a 27–13 lead, but the Ravens fought back to forge ahead 30–27 with twenty-six seconds remaining.

Josh Cribbs returned the kickoff 39 yards to the Cleveland 43-yard line. The Browns advanced the ball to the Baltimore 34-yard line with 3 seconds left. Phil Dawson came on to try a 51-yard field goal. The kick had more than enough distance, but the ball deflected off the left upright and, incredibly, onto the top of the support beam beyond the crossbar. It then ricocheted back in front of the crossbar before falling to the ground. Time ran out. It was an extraordinary sequence no observer had ever seen before. The initial ruling was that Dawson's kick was no good. The two officials beneath the goalpost saw only that the ball sprung backward and tumbled down short of the crossbar.

Players from both sides were in their respective locker rooms, thinking the game was over, that Baltimore had won, when news arrived that the game was not over. Although field goals, by rule, are not reviewable via instant replay, officials had huddled and reversed their original call—the correct decision—making Dawson's three-pointer good, thus tying the score at 30 and forcing overtime. The players returned to the field. Dawson's 33-yard field goal nearly six minutes into the extra period gave the Browns an amazing 33–30 triumph.

17. The Arizona Cardinals. The Cardinals hadn't even had a winning season in a decade. A stretch during the 2008 season in which the Cards won five of six games was the fuel behind the fire that resulted in a 9-7 finish and the championship of their weak division. Arizona was the only team in the division that had a winning record.

Kurt Warner was 401-of-598 for 4,583 yards with 30 touchdowns and 14 interceptions. Edgerrin James ran the ball 133 times for 514 yards with 3 touchdowns. Tim Hightower rushed the ball 143 times for 399 yards with 10 touchdowns and had 34 receptions for 237 yards. The Cardinals had the rarity of 3 receivers with 1,000 yards—Larry Fitzgerald had 1,431 on 96 receptions, Anquan Boldin had 1,038 on 89 catches, and Steve Breaston had 1,006 on 77 receptions.

Arizona defeated Atlanta 30–24 in a wild card game, crushed Carolina 33–13 in a divisional playoff, and beat Philadelphia 32–25 in the NFC Championship game. In the Super Bowl, played on February 1, 2009, at Raymond James Stadium in Tampa, Florida, the Cardinals met the AFC champion Pittsburgh Steelers. Down 10–0 in the second quarter, the Cardinals cut their deficit to three points when Warner completed a 1-yard touchdown pass to Ben Patrick. The Steelers took a 17–7 lead when James Harrison returned an interception 100 yards for a touchdown on the final play of the first half.

Trailing 20–7 in the fourth quarter, the Cardinals pulled to within 20–14 on a short touchdown pass from Warner to Fitzgerald. With just less than three minutes remaining, the Cards cut their deficit to 20–16 on a safety when center Justin Hartwig was penalized for holding in the Steelers' end zone. On their ensuing possession, the Cardinals took a 23–20 lead with two minutes and thirty-seven seconds left on a 64-yard touchdown pass from Warner to Fitzgerald. Ben Roethlisberger then drove the Steelers 78 yards to the winning score, his 6-yard touchdown pass to Santonio Holmes with thirty-five seconds to go. On the ensuing possession, the Cardinals advanced the ball to the Pittsburgh 44-yard line, but that was as close as they got. Pittsburgh won 27–23.

18. Andre Johnson. He did it as a member of the Houston Texans. In 2008, he had 1,575 receiving yards on a league-leading 115 receptions with 8 touchdowns. That year, in a 29–28 win over Miami on October 12, he had 10 receptions for 178 yards with a touchdown. In a 13–12 triumph over Tennessee on December 14, he had 11 catches for 207 yards with a touchdown. The next season, he had an NFL-high 1,569 receiving yards on 101 receptions with 9 touchdowns. That year, in a 34–7 victory over Seattle on December 13, he had 11 receptions for 193 yards with 2 touchdowns. In a 16–13 win over St. Louis the very next week, on December 20, he had 9 catches for 196 yards.

In his rookie season with Houston in 2003, Johnson had 66 receptions for 976 yards with 4 touchdowns. The next year, he had 79 catches for 1,142 yards with 6 touchdowns. In 2006, he led the NFL with 103 receptions. His 2011 season was shortened due to an injury, but he did help the Texans to a 10-6 record and the AFC South Division title, their first playoff berth ever. In a 31–10 wild card win over Cincinnati, he had 5 receptions for 90 yards, including a 40-yard touchdown. Despite a 20–13 loss to Baltimore in a divisional playoff, he managed 8 catches for 111 yards. The next season, he led the Texans to a 12-4 record and a second straight division championship. In a 41–28 defeat to the Patriots in a divisional playoff, he had 8 receptions for

95 yards. He played for Houston through the 2014 season. He concluded his career with Indianapolis in 2015 and Tennessee in 2016.

Overall, Johnson had 1,062 receptions for 14,185 yards with 70 touchdowns. He was picked for the Pro Bowl in 2004, 2006, from 2008 through 2010, and in 2012 and 2013.

19. Josh Cribbs. Cribbs's first touchdown return was for 100 yards late in the first quarter. His second touchdown return was for 103 yards late in the second quarter. He wound up with 269 kickoff return yards on 6 returns.

Cribbs actually had been a quarterback in college for Kent State University. He joined the Browns in 2005 as a rookie free agent and led them in kickoff returns and kickoff return yards from 2005 through 2012 and in punt returns and punt return yards from 2007 through 2012. He concluded his career playing one season for the New York Jets in 2013 and his final season with Indianapolis in 2014.

Overall, Cribbs returned 8 kickoffs—an NFL record that has since been tied—and 3 punts for touchdowns. All-time, he had 426 kickoff returns for 11,113 yards and 222 punt returns for 2,375 yards. He also played wide receiver. His best year at that position was in 2011 when he had 41 receptions for 518 yards with 4 touchdowns. He was a Pro Bowler in 2007, 2009, and 2012.

20. b. Indianapolis Colts. The Colts finished 14-2 in 2009 and won the AFC South Division title. They beat the Baltimore Ravens 20–3 in a divisional playoff and the New York Jets 30–17 in the AFC Championship game. The Super Bowl was played on February 7, 2010, at Dolphin Stadium in Miami.

The Colts had a 10–0 lead after one quarter on a 38-yard field goal by Matt Stover and a 19-yard touchdown pass from Peyton Manning to Pierre Garcon. The Saints pulled to within 10–6 at halftime on a pair of Garrett Hartley field goals from 46 and 44 yards. Early in the third quarter, they took a 13–10 lead when Drew Brees threw a 16-yard touchdown pass to Pierre Thomas. Later in the third, Indianapolis forged ahead 17–13 on a 4-yard touchdown run by Joseph Addai. Hartley's 47-yard field goal pulled New Orleans within 17–16 after three quarters. The Saints took a 24–17 lead with five minutes and forty-two seconds remaining on a short touchdown pass from Brees to Jeremy Shockey. Tracy Porter's 74-yard interception return for a touchdown with three minutes and twelve seconds to go accounted for the game's final points and shut the coffin lid on the Colts.

Brees was 32-of-39 for 288 yards. Thomas rushed the ball nine times for 30 yards and had 6 receptions for 55 yards. Reggie Bush ran the ball 5 times for 25 yards and had 4 catches for 38 yards. Marques Colston had 7 receptions for 83 yards, including a 27-yarder, while Devery Henderson had 7 catches for 63 yards.

Manning was 31-of-45 for 333 yards with an interception. Addai had 13 carries for 77 yards and 7 receptions for 58 yards. Dallas Clark had 7 catches for 86 yards, including a 27-yarder, while Austin Collie had 6 receptions for 66 yards, including a 40-yarder. Garcon caught 5 passes for 66 yards, and Reggie Wayne had 5 catches for 46 yards.

2010–2019

PRO FOOTBALL IN THE AGE OF SOCIAL MEDIA

By 2010, the nation was swamped with the NFL. The NFL Network had become almost a necessity for fans who wanted to be tuned in to everything going on with the league. The NFL Red-Zone, an offshoot of the NFL Network, allows fans to see every single touchdown during Sunday afternoon games. It is closely linked to Fantasy Football, reporting superlatives and tracking various statistical accomplishments throughout the afternoon. As for the game itself, 4,000-yard passing seasons had become the norm rather than the exception.

QUESTIONS

1. What NFC West Division team became the first ever to win a division with a losing record in 2010? *Answer on page 208.*

2. What AFC quarterback led the NFL with 4,710 passing yards in 2010? *Answer on page 209.*

3. The 2011 Green Bay Packers finished 15-1. What AFC West team beat them? *Answer on page 210.*

4. I had a total of 98 sacks as a linebacker for the Denver Broncos from 2011 through 2018. Who am I? *Answer on page 210.*

5. Peyton Manning's last season as the Indianapolis Colts' starting quarterback was 2010. Andrew Luck's first season as their starting quarterback was 2012. Who manned the Colts' quarterback position in the season in-between, 2011? *Answer on page 211.*

6. Who led the NFL with 2,097 rushing yards, the second most ever, in 2012? *Answer on page 211.*

7. What NFC North quarterback led the NFL in 2012 with 435 completions and 727 passes? *Answer on page 213.*

8. Brothers Jim Harbaugh (San Francisco 49ers) and John Harbaugh (Baltimore Ravens) opposed one another as head coaches in Super Bowl XLVII, the "Harbaugh Bowl," the only time that has ever happened. The Ravens won. What was the score? *Answer on page 213.*

   a. 33–30
   b. 37–34
   c. 34–31
   d. 34–30

9. Cleveland Browns wide receiver Josh Gordon set an NFL record in 2013 for most receiving yards in a four-game stretch with _____ from November 17 to December 8. *Answer on page 214.*

a. 574   b. 674

c. 774   d. 874

10. Who led the NFL with 8 interceptions in 2013? *Answer on page 215.*

11. What kicker led the NFL by making 96.2 percent of his field goals in 2013? *Answer on page 215.*

    a. Matt Prater

    b. Shaun Suisham

    c. Justin Tucker

    d. Dan Bailey

12. The Seattle Seahawks won their first Super Bowl by beating the _____ in Super Bowl XLVIII. *Answer on page 216.*

13. In what passing category did the Pittsburgh Steelers' Ben Roethlisberger lead the NFL in 2014? *Answer on page 217.*

14. The 2014 New England Patriots won Super Bowl XLIX, their first Super Bowl title in _____ years. *Answer on page 217.*

15. What NFC wide receiver led the NFL in 2015 with 136 receptions and 1,871 receiving yards? *Answer on page 218.*

16. Peyton Manning's final NFL game was a Super Bowl win. True or false? *Answer on page 219.*

17. The Cleveland Browns' composite record in 2016 and 2017 was _____. *Answer on page 220.*

a. 0-32   **b.** 1-31
c. 2-30   **d.** 3-29

18. The New England Patriots recovered from a 28–3 deficit to beat the _____ in Super Bowl LI. *Answer on page 221.*

19. What team did the Philadelphia Eagles defeat 41–33 in Super Bowl LII? *Answer on page 222.*

    a. New England Patriots
    b. Denver Broncos
    c. Pittsburgh Steelers
    d. Baltimore Ravens

20. When Tom Brady led New England to a 13–3 victory over the Los Angeles Rams in Super Bowl LIII, he became the only player to win six Super Bowls. With whom had he been tied at five Super Bowl wins? *Answer on page 223.*

ANSWERS

1. The Seattle Seahawks. The Seahawks finished with a 7-9 record, beating out the 7-9 St. Louis Rams on a tiebreaker. In fact, Seattle defeated the Rams 16–6 in the season finale to win the division crown. Because they won their division, the Seahawks hosted the 11-5, but wild card, New Orleans Saints in a first-round playoff game.

    Down 17–7 in the second quarter, Seattle pulled to within 17–14 when Matt Hasselbeck threw a 7-yard touchdown pass to John Carlson. Olindo Mare's 29-yard field goal tied the score. Later in the quarter, Hasselbeck hit Brandon Stokley on a 45-yard scoring strike to give the Seahawks their first lead at 24–17. It was 24–20 at halftime. In the third quarter, Mike Williams caught a 38-yard touchdown pass from Hasselbeck to stretch the Seattle lead to 31–20. Mare's 39-yard field goal made it 34–20 entering the fourth quarter. The Saints pulled within 34–30 on a 4-yard touchdown run by Julius Jones and a 21-yard field goal by Garrett Hartley. The Seahawks put the dagger to the New Orleans heart when Marshawn Lynch ran for a 67-yard touchdown and a 41–30 lead. Drew Brees threw a 6-yard touchdown pass to Devery Henderson with one minute and thirty seconds to go, but it was too little, too late in Seattle's 41–36 victory.

The next week, in a divisional playoff, the Seahawks opposed the Bears in Chicago. The Bears took a 14–0 lead after one quarter on a 58-yard touchdown pass from Jay Cutler to Greg Olsen and a short touchdown run by Chester Taylor. A 6-yard touchdown run by Cutler made the score 21–0 at halftime. Cutler scored on a 9-yard run in the third quarter to make it 28–0. The Seahawks made it 28–3 heading into the fourth quarter on Mare's 30-yard field goal. They pulled within 28–10 on a 2-yard touchdown run by Williams. The Bears put an end to any hope the visitors may have had when Cutler connected with Kellen Davis on a 39-yard touchdown pass to give Chicago a 35–10 lead. Two late touchdowns pulled the Seahawks within 35–24, but that was as close as they got and how the game ended.

2. Philip Rivers. He did it as a member of the San Diego Chargers. That season, he was 357-of-541 with 30 touchdowns and 13 interceptions. He had two 400-yard passing games that year. Despite a 27–20 loss to Seattle on September 26, he was 29-of-53 for 455 yards with 2 touchdowns and 2 interceptions. Two weeks later, on October 10, in a 35–27 loss to Oakland, he was 27-of-42 for 431 yards with 2 touchdowns. In his rookie season of 2004 and in 2005, he sat on the bench behind starter Drew Brees, but when Brees signed with New Orleans during the 2006 offseason, Rivers became the main man for the Chargers. That season, he was 284-of-460 for 3,388 yards with 22 touchdowns and 9 interceptions in leading his team to a 14-2 record and the AFC West title.

The next season, Rivers was 277-of-460 for 3,152 yards with 21 touchdowns and 15 interceptions in leading San Diego to an 11-5 record and the AFC West championship. In a 17–6 wild card playoff win over Tennessee, he was 19-of-30 for 292 yards with a touchdown and a pick. In a 28–24 divisional playoff victory over Indianapolis, he was 14-of-19 for 264 yards with 3 touchdowns and an interception. In a 21–12 loss to New England in the AFC title game, he was 19-of-37 for 211 yards with 2 interceptions.

Although he and the Chargers have not returned to the conference championship game since, Rivers has had some magnificent seasons. He passed for 4,000 yards nine other times, with a high of 4,792 in 2015, a season in which he led the league with 437 completions and 661 passes. He led San Diego/Los Angeles to the playoffs in 2008, 2009, 2013, and 2018.

Overall, Rivers has completed 4,518 of 7,000 passes for 54,656 yards with 374 touchdowns and 178 interceptions. He was a Pro Bowler in 2006, from 2009 through 2011, in 2013, and from 2016 through 2018.

3. The Kansas City Chiefs. The Packers took a 13-0 record into a December 18 meeting with the Chiefs at Arrowhead Stadium in Kansas City. The Chiefs came in with just a 5-8 record. Two Ryan Succop first-quarter field goals gave Kansas City a 6–0 halftime lead. Green Bay took a 7–6 lead in the third quarter when Aaron Rodgers threw a short touchdown pass to Donald Driver. Two more Succop field goals had the Chiefs back in the lead 12–7 in the fourth quarter. Jackie Battle's 1-yard touchdown run with four minutes and fifty-three seconds remaining made the score 19–7. Rodgers scored from 8 yards out with two minutes and four seconds left, but that was as close as the Packers got in a 19–14 defeat.

Incredibly, the Packers were ousted in their first playoff game, 37–20 at home to the New York Giants—who were just 9-7 during the regular season—in the divisional playoffs.

4. Von Miller. On my first career play from scrimmage in my rookie season on September 12, 2011, I forced a fumble

against the Oakland Raiders. That year, I had 11.5 sacks in helping Denver to the AFC West title and a playoff win over Pittsburgh. The next season, I had 18.5 sacks and helped the Broncos to a 13-3 record and the AFC West title. I had 3 sacks in both a 31–23 win over Cincinnati on November 4 and a 30–23 win over San Diego on November 18. My sack totals from 2014 through 2017 were 14, 11, 13.5, and 10. On November 24, 2013, I returned a fumble 60 yards for a touchdown in a 34–31 overtime loss to New England. That season, despite off-the-field issues and injury that shortened my season to nine games, I helped the Broncos advance to Super Bowl XLVIII. Two years later, I helped them to a 24–10 victory over the Carolina Panthers in Super Bowl 50.

I was picked for the Pro Bowl in 2011 and 2012 and from 2014 through 2018.

5. Curtis Painter, Dan Orlovsky, and Kerry Collins. The three of them shared the Colts' quarterback duties. Painter and Orlovsky were career backups for the most part. Collins had enjoyed a nice, long career but was in his final season. The 2011 Colts finished 2-14 and in last place in the AFC South. Painter was 132-of-243 for 1,541 yards with 6 touchdowns and 9 interceptions. Orlovsky, who had played a major role in the Detroit Lions' 0-16 2008 season, was 122-of-193 for 1,201 yards with 6 touchdowns and 4 interceptions. Collins was 48-of-98 for 481 yards with 2 touchdowns and a pick.

The Colts lost their first thirteen games, including a 62–7 defeat to New Orleans on October 23. Their first win came against Tennessee on December 18 by a 27–13 score. They beat the Texans the next week but fell to Jacksonville to end the season.

6. Adrian Peterson. Peterson did it as a member of the Minnesota Vikings. That yardage total came on 348 rushes. He ran for 12 touchdowns. He also had 40 receptions for 217 yards with a touchdown. That year, in a 23–14 loss to Green Bay on December 2, he had 21 rushes for 210 yards with a touchdown. Two weeks later, on December 16 in a 36–22

win over St. Louis, he ran the ball 24 times for 212 yards with a touchdown. In a regular-season-ending 37–34 victory over the Packers, he had 34 carries for 199 yards with a touchdown. Despite a 24–10 NFC Wild Card loss to Green Bay, he had 22 rushes for 99 yards.

In his rookie season of 2007 with Minnesota, Peterson rushed the ball 238 times for 1,341 yards with 12 touchdowns. He also had 19 receptions for 268 yards with a touchdown. In 2008, he ran the ball 363 times for a league-leading 1,760 yards with 10 touchdowns. He also had 21 catches for 125 yards. In a 28–27 win over Green Bay on November 9, he had 30 carries for 192 yards with a touchdown and 3 receptions for 33 yards. In a 26–14 loss to Philadelphia in a wild card playoff game, he had 20 rushes for 83 yards with both of his team's touchdowns, the first one a 40-yarder. The next season, he ran the ball 314 times for 1,383 yards with an NFL-best 18 touchdowns. He also caught 43 passes for 436 yards. Despite a 31–28 overtime loss to New Orleans in the

Adrian Peterson in action against the Eagles, December 28, 2010
Jerry Coli/Dreamstime.com

NFC Championship, he had 25 carries for 122 yards with 3 touchdowns. He also topped the thousand-yard mark in 2010, 2013, and 2015, the last year in which he helped the Vikings qualify for the playoffs. In 2017, he played for Arizona and New Orleans, and in 2018 he played for Washington. Overall, Peterson has 2,825 rushes for 13,318 yards with 106 touchdowns. He has 272 receptions for 2,223 yards with 5 touchdowns. He was a Pro Bowler from 2007 through 2010 and in 2012, 2013, and 2015.

7. Matthew Stafford. He did it as a member of the Detroit Lions. That year, he threw for 4,967 yards with 20 touchdowns and 17 interceptions. He had two 400-yard passing games. Despite a 34–31 overtime loss to Houston on November 22, he was 31-of-61 for 441 yards with 2 touchdowns. In a 31–18 loss to Atlanta on December 22, he was 37-of-56 for 443 yards with an interception. His rookie year with the Lions was in 2009 as the number-one overall draft pick out of the University of Georgia. In 2011, he led Detroit to a 10-6 record and a playoff berth. He was 421-of-663 for 5,038 yards with 41 touchdowns and 16 interceptions. In a 31–17 loss to New Orleans on December 4, he was 31-of-44 for 408 yards with a touchdown and a pick. In a regular-season–ending 45–41 defeat to Green Bay on New Year's Day 2012, he was 36-of-59 for 520 yards with 5 touchdowns and 2 interceptions. In a 45–28 wild card loss to the Saints, he was 28-of-43 for 380 yards with 3 touchdowns and 2 interceptions. He passed for 4,000 yards every season from 2013 through 2017. He led the Lions to the playoffs in 2014 and 2016.

Overall, Stafford has completed 3,372 of 5,405 passes for 38,526 yards with 237 touchdowns and 129 interceptions. He was a Pro Bowler in 2014.

8. c. 34–31. The 49ers finished 11-4-1 in winning the NFC West Division title. They beat Green Bay and Atlanta in the playoffs to advance to the Super Bowl. The Ravens were 10-6 and won the AFC North Division title. They defeated Indianapolis, Denver, and New England in the playoffs to reach the Super Bowl.

The Super Bowl was played on February 3, 2013, at the Mercedez-Benz Superdome in New Orleans. The Ravens took a 7–0 first-quarter lead when Joe Flacco completed a 13-yard touchdown pass to Anquan Boldin. The 49ers cut it to 7–3 after one quarter on a 36-yard field goal by David Akers. Touchdown passes from Flacco to Dennis Pitta (1 yard) and Jacoby Jones (56 yards) ballooned the Baltimore lead to 21–3. Another field goal by Akers, from 27 yards, made the score 21–6 at halftime.

Jones returned the second-half kickoff 108 yards for a touchdown and a 28–6 Ravens' lead. The 'Niners pulled to within 28–23 after three quarters on a 31-yard touchdown pass from Colin Kaepernick to Michael Crabtree, a 6-yard touchdown run by Frank Gore, and a 34-yard field goal by Akers. Justin Tucker kicked a 19-yard field goal as Baltimore stretched its lead to 31–23. Kaepernick scored from 15 yards out, but San Francisco failed on the two-point conversion, leaving the score 31–29. Tucker's 38-yard field goal with 4:19 left upped the Ravens' lead to 34–29. Ravens punter Sam Koch took an intentional safety by running the ball out of the end zone with four seconds to go. The Ravens went on to win 34–31.

9. c. 774. Not surprisingly, the bumbling Browns lost all four games. Gordon had 125 yards on 5 receptions in a 41–20 defeat at Cincinnati on November 17. In a 27–11 home loss to Pittsburgh on November 24, he had 237 yards on 14 receptions. In a 32–28 home defeat to Jacksonville on December 1, he had 261 yards on 10 receptions. In a 27–26 loss at New England on December 8, he had 151 yards on 7 receptions. Despite missing the first two games of the season due to off-the-field problems, Gordon was the team leader in receptions (87), receiving yards (1,646), and touchdown catches (9). His yardage total was tops in the entire NFL, earning him a trip to the Pro Bowl.

Gordon had been chosen in the second round of the 2012 supplemental draft. That year, his rookie season, he had 50 receptions for both a team-best 805 yards and 5 touchdowns. In spite of his magnificent 2013 season, his off-the-field issues resurfaced and caused him to miss eleven games the next year, got him suspended for the entire 2015 season, and kept him out of the 2016 season. He rejoined the Browns late in the 2017 season and then was traded to the Patriots early in the 2018 season. His off-the-field problems caused him to leave the Patriots with two games left on the schedule.

Overall, Gordon has 220 receptions for 3,826 yards with 19 touchdowns.

10. Richard Sherman. Sherman accomplished the feat as a member of the Seattle Seahawks. He totaled 125 return yards off of those picks, including a 58-yarder for a touchdown off a Matt Schaub pass late in the fourth quarter that helped Seattle to a 23–20 overtime win against the Houston Texans. Late that season, Sherman had two straight 2-interception games—a 23–0 victory over the New York Giants on December 15 and a 17–10 loss to Arizona on December 22. He helped the Seahawks win Super Bowl XLVIII that year. The next season, he had 4 interceptions in helping Seattle return to the Super Bowl, but this time the Seahawks lost. In his rookie season of 2011 with Seattle, he had 4 interceptions. The next year, he had 8 interceptions, including a 19-yard pick-six that helped the Seahawks to a 58–0 win over the Cardinals. He joined the San Francisco 49ers in 2018.

Overall, Sherman has 32 interceptions and 395 interception return yards. He was a Pro Bowler from 2013 through 2016.

11. Matt Prater. He did it as a member of the Denver Broncos. He connected on 25 of 26 field-goal attempts. His longest field goal that year was a 64-yarder in a 51–28 victory over the Tennessee Titans on December 8. That kick set an NFL record, breaking the old mark of 63 yards. He helped the Broncos advance all the way to Super Bowl XLVIII.

Prater was not even drafted out of the University of Central Florida. He spent his rookie season in 2007 with Atlanta and then Denver. In 2010, he hit on 16 of 18 field-goal tries for an 88.9 percentage. In 2015, he made good on 22 of 24 field-goal attempts, a success rate of 91.7 percent. He has kicked several field goals of 59 and 58 yards. He joined the Detroit Lions during the 2014 season.

Overall, Prater has made 274 of 327 field-goal attempts for 83.8 percent. He was a Pro Bowler in 2013 and 2016.

12. Denver Broncos. The 2013 Seahawks finished 13-3 and won the NFC West Division title. They defeated New Orleans and San Francisco in the playoffs to advance to the Super Bowl. The Broncos were also 13-3 in winning the AFC West Division championship. They beat San Diego and New England in the playoffs to reach the Super Bowl.

The Super Bowl was played on February 2, 2014, at MetLife Stadium in East Rutherford, New Jersey. Seattle dominated from the very start. A safety and 2 field goals had the Seahawks ahead 8–0 after one quarter. In the second quarter, Marshawn Lynch had a 1-yard touchdown run to increase the Seattle lead to 15–0. Later in the quarter, Malcolm Smith returned an interception of a Peyton Manning pass 69 yards for a touchdown and a 22–0 Seahawks' halftime advantage. Percy Harvin returned the second-half kickoff 87 yards for a touchdown to make the score 29–0. Later in the third quarter, Russell Wilson threw a 23-yard touchdown pass to Jermaine Kearse for a 36–0 Seattle lead. The Broncos avoided a shutout when Manning hit Demaryius Thomas on a 14-yard touchdown pass as the third quarter ended to make the score 36–8. For good measure, Wilson completed a 10-yard touchdown pass to Doug Baldwin for the game's final points in a 43–8 Seahawks' rout.

Wilson was 18-of-25 for 206 yards. He ran the ball 3 times for 26 yards. Harvin had 2 rushes for 45 yards, including a 30-yarder. Baldwin had 5 receptions for 66 yards, including a 37-yarder, while Kearse had 4 catches for 65 yards, including a 24-yarder. Manning was 34-of-49 for 280 yards with 2 interceptions. Thomas had 13 receptions for 118 yards, including a 23-yarder, and Wes Welker caught 8 passes for 84 yards, including a 22-yarder.

13. Yards. Roethlisberger threw for 4,952 yards and was 408-of-608 with 32 touchdowns and 9 interceptions. In a 51–34 victory over Indianapolis on October 26, he was 40-of-49 for 522 yards with 6 touchdowns. The very next week, on November 2, in a 43–23 win over Baltimore, he repeated his accomplishment from the week before with 6 touchdown passes. He was 25-of-37 for 340 yards. In a 35–32 loss to New Orleans on November 30, he was 32-of-58 for 435 yards with 2 touchdowns and 2 interceptions. In a 30–17 loss to the Ravens in an AFC Wild Card Playoff, he was 31-of-45 for 334 yards with a touchdown and 2 picks.

In his rookie season with Pittsburgh in 2004, Roethlisberger was 196-of-295 for 2,621 yards with 17 touchdowns and 11 interceptions. He led the Steelers to a 15-1 record and all the way to the AFC Championship game. He had other 4,000-yard passing seasons in 2009, 2011, 2013, 2017, and 2018, the latter in which he eclipsed 5,000 yards. He has led the Steelers to ten playoff berths and three Super Bowls, the first two of which they won in 2005 and 2008.

Overall, Roethlisberger has completed 4,616 of 7,168 passes for 56,194 yards with 363 touchdowns and 190 interceptions. He was a Pro Bowler in 2007, 2011, and from 2014 through 2017.

14. 10. The Patriots last won the Super Bowl in 2004 when they won Super Bowl XXXIX over Philadelphia. Since then, they appeared in two Super Bowls but lost them both to the New York Giants. In 2014, New England finished 12-4 and won the AFC East Division. They beat Baltimore 35–31 in a thrilling divisional playoff and then crushed Indianapolis 45–7 in the AFC Championship game en route to the Super Bowl, in which they opposed the NFC champion Seattle Seahawks.

The Super Bowl was played on February 1, 2015, before 70,288 fans at the University of Phoenix Stadium in Glendale, Arizona. After a scoreless first quarter, the Patriots took a 7–0 second-quarter lead when Tom Brady completed an 11-yard touchdown pass to Brandon LaFell. The Seahawks tied the score on a 3-yard touchdown run by Marshawn Lynch. The Patriots took a 14–7 lead on a 22-yard touchdown pass from Brady to Rob Gronkowski. The Seahawks tied the score 14–14 at halftime on an 11-yard touchdown pass from Russell Wilson to Chris Matthews. Seattle went ahead 24–14 after three quarters on a 27-yard field goal by Steven Hauschka and a short touchdown pass from Wilson to Doug Baldwin. About halfway through the fourth quarter, Brady threw a 3-yard touchdown pass to Danny Amendola to pull New England within 24–21.

After a three-and-out by the Seahawks, Brady led his team on a 68-yard drive that culminated with a 3-yard touchdown pass from Brady to Julian Edelman with two minutes and two seconds to go as the Patriots forged ahead 28–24. Wilson drove the Seahawks all the way to the New England 1-yard line with 26 seconds left. He threw a pass intended for Ricardo Lockette, but Malcolm Butler intercepted it, resulting in victory for the Patriots.

15. Julio Jones. He achieved the feat as a member of the Atlanta Falcons. He caught 8 touchdown passes that year. In a 39–28 victory over Dallas on September 27, he had 12 receptions for 164 yards with 2 touchdowns. In a 20–13 win over Carolina on December 27, he had 9 catches for 178 yards with a touchdown.

In his rookie season of 2011 with Atlanta, Jones had 54 receptions for 959 yards with 8 touchdowns. In 2012, he caught 79 passes for 1,198 yards with 10 touchdowns. In a 28–24 defeat to San Francisco in the NFC Championship game that year, he had 11 receptions for 182 yards with 2 touchdowns, including a 46-yarder. In 2014, he had 104 catches for 1,593 yards with 6 touchdowns. In a 43–37 loss to Green Bay on December 8, he caught 11 passes for 259 yards with a touchdown. He exceeded 1,400 receiving yards in both 2016 and 2017 in helping the Falcons to the playoffs both years, including a Super Bowl appearance in 2016. He totaled almost 1,700 receiving yards in 2018.

Overall, Jones has 698 receptions for 10,731 yards with 51 touchdowns. He was picked for the Pro Bowl in 2012 and from 2014 through 2018.

16. True. Manning's last game was as a member of the Denver Broncos in a 24–10 victory over the Carolina Panthers in Super Bowl 50 on February 7, 2016, at Levi's Stadium in Santa Clara, California. The 2015 Broncos finished 12-4 and won the AFC West. They beat Pittsburgh and New England in the playoffs to reach the Super Bowl. The Panthers were 15-1 and won the NFC South. They defeated Seattle and Arizona in the playoffs to advance to the Super Bowl.

In the Super Bowl, the Broncos took a 3–0 first-quarter lead on a 34-yard field goal by Brandon McManus. Malik Jackson recovered a fumble by one of his teammates in the end zone for a touchdown that gave Denver a 10–0 lead after one quarter. Jonathan Stewart's 1-yard touchdown run in the second quarter pulled Carolina to within 10–7. Two McManus field goals later, the Broncos had a 16–7 lead in the fourth quarter. Graham Gano's 39-yard field goal brought the Panthers within 16–10, but with 3:08 remaining, C. J. Anderson scored from 2 yards out to expand the Broncos' lead to 24–10, and that was the game's final points.

Manning was 13-of-23 for 141 yards with an interception. Anderson had 23 rushes for 90 yards, including a 34-yarder. Emmanuel Sanders had 6 receptions for 83 yards, including a 25-yarder. For Carolina, Cam Newton was 18-of-41 for 265 yards with a pick. He also ran the ball 6 times for 45 yards. Corey Brown had 4 receptions for 80 yards, including a 42-yarder, while Ted Ginn had 4 catches for 74 yards, including a 45-yarder. Greg Olsen caught 4

Peyton Manning prepares to throw a pass against the 49ers in a preseason game, August 29, 2015.
Library of Congress

passes for 41 yards, and Devin Funchess had 2 receptions for 40 yards, including a 24-yarder.

17. b. 1-31. The 2016 Browns finished 1-15. The 2017 Browns were 0-16, just the second NFL team to sink to those depths (the 2008 Detroit Lions were the other). Hue Jackson was the head coach both seasons.

The 2016 Browns scored 264 points and yielded 452 points. They began the season with a 29–10 loss to the Philadelphia Eagles. The Eagles were led by Carson Wentz, whom the Browns passed over by trading the second overall pick in the 2016 draft to the Eagles. Wentz was 22-of-37 for 278 yards with 2 touchdowns in his NFL debut. That year, the Browns certainly had their share of blowout losses, but they also had several close defeats, including a 25–20 loss to Baltimore, a 30–24 overtime loss to Miami, and a 31–28 loss to the New York Jets. The Browns lost their first fourteen games before finally notching victory number one, 20–17 over San Diego at home on Christmas Eve when Josh Lambo missed a potential game-tying 44-yard field goal as time expired.

The 2017 Browns scored 234 points and gave up 410 points. Like the 2016 Browns, they had several games in which they were beaten badly but also a handful of games that came down the last few minutes, including a season-opening 21–18 loss to Pittsburgh, a 12–9 overtime defeat to Tennessee, and a 27–21 overtime loss to Green Bay.

18. Atlanta Falcons. The 2016 Patriots finished 14-2 and won the AFC East. They defeated Houston and Pittsburgh in the playoffs to advance to the Super Bowl. The Falcons were 11-5 in winning the NFC South. They beat Seattle and Green Bay in the playoffs to reach the Super Bowl.

The Super Bowl was played on February 5, 2017, at NRG Stadium in Houston. After a scoreless first quarter, the Falcons erupted for 3 touchdowns in the second quarter. Devonta Freeman scored on a 5-yard run, Matt Ryan threw a 19-yard touchdown pass to Austin Hooper, and Robert Alford intercepted a Tom Brady pass and returned the ball 82 yards for a touchdown and a 21–0 Atlanta lead. Stephen Gostkowski's 41-yard field goal pulled the Patriots within 21–3 at halftime and gave them at least some hope. That hope was seemingly squashed when Ryan hit Tevin Coleman on a 6-yard touchdown pass about midway through the third quarter to increase the Falcons' lead to 28–3.

Never count Tom Brady out, though.

Brady completed a 5-yard touchdown pass to James White to pull his team within 28–9 after three quarters. A 33-yard field goal by Gostkowski made the score 28–12. Brady threw a 6-yard touchdown pass to Danny Amendola, and with the two-point conversion, the Pats were within 28–20 with five minutes and fifty-six seconds remaining. White scored from a yard out with fifty-seven seconds left to make the score 28–26. Brady passed to Amendola for the two-point conversion that tied the score at 28. The game went into overtime, becoming the first NFL championship contest to go into overtime since the famous 1958 Baltimore Colts–New York Giants game. On the first overtime possession, Brady drove the Patriots 75 yards to the winning score, White's 2-yard touchdown run just less than four minutes into the extra period. The Patriots won 34–28. It marked the only time in NFL postseason history that a team leading by 17 points or more at the start of the fourth quarter went on to lose the game.

19. a. New England Patriots. The 2017 Eagles won the franchise's first NFL championship in 57 years. The Eagles finished 13-3 and won the NFC East. They defeated Atlanta and Minnesota in the playoffs to reach the Super Bowl. Their quarterback in the postseason was backup Nick Foles, who replaced the injured Carson Wentz during the division-clinching win over the Los Angeles Rams on December 10. The Patriots were also 13-3 in winning the AFC East. They beat Tennessee and Jacksonville in the playoffs en route to the Super Bowl.

The Super Bowl was played on February 4, 2018, at U.S. Bank Stadium in Minneapolis. The teams traded field goals early on, and then Foles completed a 34-yard touchdown pass to Alshon Jeffery to give the Eagles a 9–3 lead after one quarter. In the second quarter, LeGarrette Blount's 21-yard touchdown run upped the Eagles' lead to 15–3. A 45-yard Stephen Gostkowski field goal and a 26-yard touchdown run by James White pulled the Patriots to within 15–12. On a trick play, Foles caught a 1-yard touchdown pass from tight end Trey Burton, making Foles the first quarterback ever to catch a touchdown pass in a Super Bowl and giving the Eagles a 22–12 halftime lead.

In the third quarter, Foles's 22-yard touchdown pass to Corey Clement was sandwiched between a pair of touchdown passes by Tom Brady, the first a 5-yarder to Rob

The 199th pick in the 2000 NFL Draft, Tom Brady has led the Patriots to nine Super Bowls and six championships.

Jerry Coli/Dreamstime.com

Gronkowski, and the second a 26-yarder to Chris Hogan. The Eagles led 29–26 entering the fourth quarter. After Jake Elliott's 42-yard field goal upped their lead to 32–26, Gronkowski caught a short touchdown pass from Brady with nine minutes and twenty-two seconds remaining to give New England its only lead of the night, 33–32. Foles hit Zach Ertz on an 11-yard touchdown pass as Philadelphia forged ahead 38–33 with two minutes and twenty-one seconds to go. Elliott kicked a 46-yard field goal with one minute and five seconds left for the game's final points.

20. Charles Haley. Haley was on Super Bowl–winning teams with San Francisco in 1988 and 1989 and Dallas in 1992, 1993, and 1995. Brady's 2018 Patriots won the AFC East with an 11-5 record. Many observers were counting the Pats out, opining that the forty-one-year-old Brady was well past his prime. But in a 41–28 home win over the Los Angeles Chargers in the divisional playoffs, Brady was 34-of-44 for 343 yards with a touchdown. In a 37–31 overtime triumph at Kansas City in the AFC title game, he was 30-of-46 for 348 yards with a touchdown and two interceptions.

In the Super Bowl win over the Rams, played on February 3, 2019, at Mercedez-Benz Stadium in Atlanta, Brady was just 21-of-35 for 262 yards with an interception on his first pass of the game. He rebounded, though, to lead two clutch fourth-quarter scoring drives of 69 and 72 yards to clinch the victory.

ACKNOWLEDGMENTS

I would like to thank Niels Aaboe of Lyons Press for giving me the opportunity to write this book and everyone else there for their assistance.

REFERENCES

CBSsports.com. "NFL ratings go up: Here were the five most-watched regular season games of the 2018 season." January 9, 2019.

The First Fifty Years: The Story of the National Football League. New York: Ridge Press, 1969.

Fischer, David. *The Super Bowl: The First Fifty Years of America's Greatest Game.* New York: Sports Publishing, 2015.

Gordon, Roger. *So You Think You're a Cleveland Browns Fan? Stars, Stats, Records, and Memories for True Diehards.* New York: Sports Publishing, 2017.

Pro-Football-Reference.com

Roberts, Randy and David Welky, eds. *The Steelers Reader.* Pittsburgh: University of Pittsburgh Press, 2003.